Game Changer

Southern Yellow Pine
Publishing

Paul Frase and Alison Rockett

Published by:
Southern Yellow Pine (SYP) Publishing
4351 Natural Bridge Rd.
Tallahassee, FL 32305

www.syppublishing.com

The contents and opinions expressed in this book do not necessarily reflect the views and opinions of Southern Yellow Pine Publishing, nor does the mention of brands or trade names constitute endorsement.

ISBN-13: 978-1-59616-120-7
ISBN-13: ePub 978-1-59616-121-4
ISBN-13: Kindle 978-1-59616-122-1

Library of Congress Control Number: 2022949227

BigStockphoto.com: 299673487
Interior photos courtesy of Paul Frase and Alison Rockett

Front Cover Design: Kurtis Loftus

Praise for Frase and Rockett

"Paul Frase and Alison Rockett have dedicated their lives to finding a cure to the cruel disease that afflicted their son Joshua. I never met Joshua, but I have known Paul and Alison for years—and I marvel at their courage and determination. They have channeled their trauma into hope, a heartbreaking diagnosis into action. They are inspirations and their story is a testament to the indomitability of love."

Jeremy Schaap, ESPN, eleven-time Emmy Award winner

"The story of Joshua Miles Frase is nothing short of a miracle. Joshua's life, and the tenacity and fortitude shown by his parents, are catalysts that have pushed science to find a cure for an ultra-rare disease. Joshua's story will inspire you to dream and encourage you to reach beyond perceived boundaries. In my opinion, this is a MUST read!

Stuart Epperson, co-founder and chairman of Salem Communications

"Frase and Rockett have written a brilliant, honest memoir profound in its ability to raise you up and cast you down. I am haunted by the line "My son, my son." But ultimately, it is a story of tremendous courage and faith, a story every parent should read."

Tim Green, American Author and former NFL player

Great young man and gave his all. Game Changer for sure! God knows!!!! R

Ronnie Lott, Hall of Fame NFL

Table of Contents

Forward

I am convinced that words cannot fully articulate or capture Joshua's impact nor entirely describe him. They merely grant one a general picture of who he is. I have come to believe, as Joshua taught me through many of his inherent attributes, that great leaders, people of destiny, are not born but are made. They do, however, have innate traits that set them apart very early. I also strongly believe that Joshua's legacy and impact will span far beyond what we currently envision. His "Map" is just the tip of the iceberg. We love you all and God bless.

Nkumu Bolinga Mandungu
Major, USAF
Joshua's Uncle

"The foundation's early work and technology in regenerative medicine has been translated into larger indications such as Parkinsons, Cancer, and other monogenic disorders. Joshua's life was not in vain."

Alison Rockett
Joshua's Mother

CHAPTER 1

ON A MISSION
Alison

Walking through the Jacksonville airport, my mind was racing, mentally reviewing my checklist. I couldn't afford a single mistake. Emotions rolled over me like waves at the ocean, and I had just enough time in between to catch my breath before each crest. Moments of clouded and hazy vision were followed by bursts of intense clarity. Every cell in my body seemed to experience these extremes all at once.

The life of my thirteen-year-old son depended on the success of this odyssey.

I passed through security and sat down on the cold metal bench to put my shoes back on. Standing up, I grabbed my bag and purse, along with my heavy winter jacket, and headed for the gate. Although this was a nice 67-degree day in northern Florida, the temperature where I was going would be below zero. Saskatoon is like that in December.

This was not a ski vacation. I was on a mission. It was part of a grueling larger journey that my husband, Paul, and I began the day our son was born. Wherever that journey took us, both of us were fully committed to seeing it through until the end, come what may.

I was going to the Canadian province of Saskatchewan to see a farmer named Vic and his wife, Karen, and their dog. Nibs was a playful chocolate lab who loved to run wild on her farm, corralling horses, and chasing jackrabbits in the fields. Nibs and I would become kindred spirits. Though we had never met, our stories were already interwoven. Our shared DNA tied us together forever. Nibs would be a gift of immeasurable love.

My son's life depended on her.

CHAPTER 2

BOY MEETS GIRL
Paul

Walking into the Sportsman's Bar that afternoon, I knew I was near the top of my game. At twenty-six, if everything went according to plan, I was about to start my fourth season in the National Football League (NFL) as a defensive lineman for the New York Jets. The only problem was that I was no longer in control of that plan.

The previous season, a bout of Graves's disease nearly cost me my highly coveted position in the NFL. For each of the previous three years, I held one of only about 240 positions in the world open to defensive lineman in the league. The reason I kept my job despite the thyroid disorder was because I performed extremely well in my second year, racking up the most tackles on the defensive line for the team. It didn't hurt that my salary, by NFL standards, didn't cost the Jets a lot of money.

I knew during training camp that I was "on the bubble" and would have to fight to stay on the roster. Countless hours in the weight room and on the practice field helped me regain the thirty-six pounds I'd lost to Graves the previous spring. It wasn't guaranteed, but I knew I was making a strong run at rejoining the team for the 1991 season.

Preseason training camp was physically brutal and psychologically unsettling. To ease the stress, my teammate Marvin Washington and I went out for a drink in Freeport, Long Island. We picked up a game of doubles billiards in a bar right on the canal. It was August 21, just thirty-six hours before the final cut-down to fifty-three players. Try as I might, I couldn't focus on billiards while my fate rested in the hands of my coaches.

It got even more difficult to focus when a girl with long, dark auburn hair walked in. I can still remember the green blouse and black shorts that she was wearing. Shaun, the guy I was playing against, addressed this gorgeous vision casually: "Hey, Sis, what's up?" She walked right past me, without a glance, until she knelt to pet her brother's Golden Retriever. The dog, named Lobster, was the mascot of the bar.

At 6'5" and 263 pounds, I stood out in a crowd. Once she noticed her brother was playing pool with a stranger, she began her rather thorough examination of my body. The NFL owned every bit of my toned and tweaked physique. I caught her attention without even saying a word. She finished her conversation with her brother and left the bar. Before she closed the door behind her, the beauty glanced over her shoulder to see if I was eyeing her. I was. After she went out into the night, I asked Shaun "Was that really your sister?" Shaun replied, "Yeah, why? You want her number?" Breaking through my shy disposition, I quickly replied, "Yes, I do!"

Her name was Alison.

Why Marvin and I chose that bar or that guy to shoot pool with on that particular night lends itself to a theme in this story. There are no coincidences in life. Alison never planned on being in Freeport, New York that night.

Born and raised in Long Island, she was living in Los Angeles, having just left her job as an assistant to the personnel manager for Guns N' Roses. At twenty-seven, she was already known as the person to hire to get things done. She was waiting for a call from the Billboard Music Awards to become an assistant producer. This trip was supposed to be a quick visit home to decompress. Life was wonderful in LA. Alison's career was gaining momentum, and everything was going according to plan.

And then one night, a few days into her visit, Alison was driving her friend's Grand Wagoneer on the south shore of Long Island. She was stopped at a red light when a drunk driver traveling around sixty miles an hour crashed into the jeep. The vehicle was totaled, and Alison received extreme whiplash and a herniated disk in her lower back. She was bedridden for weeks. I met her while she was still on the mend.

A couple of days later, my professional anxiety was over. I was awarded a roster spot on the 1991 New York Jets football team. I went to the dresser and grabbed the crumpled napkin on which I'd hastily jotted down her number and called her.

When I got to her door the night of our first date, she took me back to her mother's beautiful garden which covered the one-acre lot. There, Alison introduced me to Elsie Rockett, a five-foot three-inch spitfire of a Long Island woman. Until meeting her, I had never been asked to pass the "Sault" and "Peppa."

Elsie was seated on one of her white painted iron chairs under an arbor covered with grapes. She was enjoying an iced tea with one of her neighbors. Alison introduced me, and the interrogation began. I learned quickly that Elsie did not dwell on small talk for very long. Elsie's first inspection of me had uncovered that I was a pastor's kid and shared spiritual beliefs with Alison, at least on paper.

Alison and I headed toward Jones Beach Boardwalk for a friendly game of miniature golf. Gentleman that I am, I insisted that Alison go first on every hole. Frankly, this had nothing to do with the nicely fitted sailor pants that Alison was sporting! After Alison handed me a thorough beating on the course, we strolled the boardwalk, talking about life. We were so caught up in the whirlwind of our own lives, that the first date was surprisingly very introspective, pleasant, and casual. We spent nearly ten hours together.

The verdict? We thought fondly of each other, but she was going back to LA in a few weeks, and neither of us was interested in a long-distance relationship. We ended the evening without a kiss or a hug, and neither of us thought we would go out again.

Just before saying goodnight, however, I asked what Alison was doing that Friday. She was going to church with her mother to hear an out-of-town speaker. Having not gone to church even once in my three years on Long Island, I asked if I could join them. Alison said, "Of course!" So, we ended up with a second date of sorts, even though we seemed uninterested in getting involved romantically.

A spark ignited that Friday evening, and after ending the night with a brief kiss, we saw each other every day for the next ten weeks. Two and a half months into our whirlwind relationship, Alison returned to Los Angeles… to retrieve her belongings.

We quickly became inseparable. Life was fun together and we thought we understood one another. We had a common faith, and we'd both lived through enough to know what we didn't want in a life partner. Four months after we met in the bar, on New Year's Eve, I knelt before her and asked Alison to be my bride. She said yes.

The wedding day, October sixteenth, came around quickly. I was making plays on the field, and in the stands, the New York fans were as loyal as ever, shouting: "J-E-T-S, JETS, JETS, JETS!"

When the big day arrived, Coach Bruce Coslet kindly allowed me to leave the practice field thirty minutes early to shower and change for my wedding downtown. But my best man, Pat Kelly, would not have the same luxury. Returning to the locker room, by then buzzing with fifty-two other men preparing for a couple of days off during the grueling season, I got dressed. To my dismay, shaving cream squirted out from my dress shoes all over my pants as I inserted my foot. Dennis Byrd, the clown of the team, had pulled off yet another locker room prank. My teammates roared with laughter, but I was not amused, muttering, "Not funny, Dennis, not funny." Dennis and the rest of the gang thought otherwise, of course. Pat showered quickly and off we rushed to the waiting limo.

It wasn't long before the limo dropped us in front of Park Avenue United Methodist Church. Rushing to the front of the church, we took our place in the stairwell to wait for the rest of the groomsmen. Right there, before Alison arrived, Pat, the class clown at Syracuse, took it upon himself to counsel me, mostly in jest. "It's not too late to call this off. It's a life commitment. You sure you want to go through with this, Paul?" As the unwanted recipient of many of his pranks in college, on this day I instantly thought of a chance for retribution.

Pointing to the tiny microphone pinned to my lapel and the transmitter clipped to my belt, I told Pat that everyone in the church had heard his plea for my sanity, including Alison and her family. Pat was devastated. Finally, I burst out laughing, saying, "I finally gotcha!"

The fairy tale wedding went off without a hitch at the Burden Mansion on 5th Ave, on the west side of Central Park, accompanied by an eighteen-piece orchestra. Alison and I floated through the night, meeting our friends later for a nightcap before enjoying a two-day mini honeymoon. I had to be back on the practice field on Monday morning. The following week, Al Michaels of *Monday Night Football* kiddingly accused me of being a "big spender" for taking my new bride on a two-day honeymoon in New York.

Sadly, the Jets didn't make the playoffs that season. After the last game, Alison and I packed up from our rented house on the Long Island shore to head down to Dallas, where we planned to live during the off season. A former teammate from Syracuse, Daryl Johnston, was playing for the Cowboys and lived in Coppell near the team training facility. Daryl offered to put us up in his house while we were looking for a home of our own. We welcomed his offer, and in the spring of 1992, we found a nice place not more than a mile from Daryl's house.

Daryl also invited me to train with him during the off season at the famed Valley Ranch, the team training facility just a mile down the road from us in Coppell. Mike Woicik, the weight coach from our playing days at Syracuse, was the head weight trainer for the Cowboys. During the off season, Mike would run us until we dropped and then run us again, just like old times.

Each spring, before the beginning of training camp in July, Alison and I took a vacation to luxurious resorts in the Caribbean. By the time our kids came along, we knew the islands like the backs of our hands. We stayed where we wanted and spent money however we wished, eating great food, relaxing by the turquoise water, and finding adventures wherever they could be had. Life for a young married couple in the NFL was exactly what you might expect—a carefree whirlwind of luxury. We were living quite comfortably, but only on the surface. We had enough money to never experience any problems and enough activity to never have to depend on each other. It was a glorious and flippant season in life.

It would soon come to a screeching halt.

CHAPTER 3

WHEN LIFE TURNS ON A DIME: THE EARLY YEARS
Alison

Spring of 1994...

Have you ever noticed that death and life seem to go hand in hand? Perhaps it's to help us cope with loss or to bring hope when everything around is bleak with sorrow; either way, it can be lifesaving.

The Texas sky was sparkling with all the hope of summer the day my phone rang with the news. It was my mom. I could barely decipher her words through the sobs. As she worked through the details, I managed to string together sentences. He was sick yesterday. That hernia from last year dislodged. He didn't make it to the hospital. My father was here one day and gone the next, without a single clue that his life here on earth was coming to an end. As the only daughter of a larger-than-life man, this was a devastating blow to me. My world stopped spinning. What I knew to be true about life changed in a moment. It was too soon. It was too hard. It was too much. I was on a plane the next day headed home to a reality I didn't know how to face. Paul was already in NY getting ready for a training camp. Paul had joined my mother and brothers in the hospital as soon as he'd heard the news.

Two weeks later, after all the arrangements had been made, family had come and gone, and life for everybody else returned to normal. Paul and I conceived Joshua. I always say it was my father's last gift to me, his blessing from above; a son who possessed the strength, character, and wit of a grandfather he'd never meet. Carrying my son in my womb gave me a sense of purpose and strength to rise above the grief I experienced from the passing of my father.

It was a pregnancy split between two states. We began in Dallas where I met with my initial OBGYN for that glorious visit where you hear your child's heartbeat the first time. Naturally, Paul and I both fell in love with that little speck on the ultrasound screen. There was a shift happening deep inside of me. I was no longer floating along, untethered in the world. From the very beginning, even within my womb, my son anchored me. Over time, he would pull me so thoroughly into his orbit that we would operate as one unit and I would know his needs with just a glance in his direction.

The next time I got to see his face on a sonogram I was twenty-two weeks pregnant and in New York City. That was the day we learned we were having a boy. During the ultrasound, the technician noticed that there was possible intrauterine growth retardation, meaning the baby's head was normal size but his body wasn't gaining weight in proportion. My OBGYN assured us that 95 percent of the time the things people worry about from sonograms and amniocentesis testing never present genetically at birth. He assured us there was nothing to worry about. I trusted his judgment, but I added protein shakes in between meals to make sure my baby received enough nutrients, just in case.

Paul finished his seventh year with the New York Jets on Christmas Eve in a loss against the Houston Oilers. With the season behind us, and me being thirty-four weeks pregnant, we were ready to get back to Dallas and focus on the birth of our first-born. First on the agenda, he needed a name. Our hearts settled on Joshua Miles Frase, a little baby destined to be a born leader whose faith would never waver. In retrospect, we realized the name I'd loved for years had a powerful connection to the story of Joshua in the Old Testament, and that our son would face numerous giants.

Standard procedure called for a routine check with my Dallas OBGYN upon our return to Texas, which I dutifully fulfilled. It went off without a hitch, yet I had a strong premonition that I needed to change OBGYNs. It was nothing more than a gut feeling, the first of many that would save Joshua's life. A few phone calls later and a friend who had a business promoting doctors connected me with Dr. Myra Thompson. Her wonderful demeanor put me instantly at ease as she reviewed all the facts of the pregnancy. Within minutes of meeting her, I knew that she was the right doctor to deliver my son.

Following the natural course of appointments, I was at my thirty-eight-week checkup when Dr. Thompson announced that Joshua was still in a breech position. She made a quick referral to a Maternal Fetal medicine specialist who attempted to flip Joshua. If you've never had that happen to you, I assure you, it's an experience most women would happily forego. The doctor greased my belly and attempted to turn him, while I grabbed onto Paul with all of my might and braced for the painful procedure. No matter how many times the doctor was able to get Joshua to flip, he would flip right back into the breach position.

At the end of the procedure, the doctor looked up at us, his face etched with concern and said, "This child could have multiple sclerosis." His words sunk in and I truly entertained his words for a few seconds, but I shrugged them off instantly. Not me. That could never happen to me. I was fastidious about my health and even more so while pregnant. Surely, I would have the healthiest of children. Either way, we were headed for a cesarean—and soon. Our doctors, by now plural, wanted him out, and they wanted him out now.

As the sun rose early on February 2, I climbed into the passenger seat of my Audi sedan. My mother was in the back situated next to a carefully installed brand new car seat, and Paul was at the wheel. We were headed to the hospital. Excitement and anticipation coursed through every vein in my body. By the end of the day, no longer would I just be Alison, wife to Paul, daughter of Elsie and Jerry; the feisty girl from Long Island. I would also be Alison, Joshua's mother. The enormity of the day consumed me, and I began to center myself on the life-altering task ahead. Today would change everything.

All preparations complete, they wheeled me into the operating room where Dr. Thompson was there with a colleague. Off to the side, finishing last minute preparations was Carol, a soft-spoken woman of God—as I would later witness—who was my nurse for the day. Classical music was floating through the air of the surgical suite, and I couldn't help but notice it was a beautiful setting; the perfect atmosphere for my son to enter the world. Everybody was calm and relaxed. They hung a sheet just above my belly and Paul took his place at my head, video camera in hand. My mother was at the foot of the bed. During the C-section, I was absolutely amazed at how calm the procedure was. There was no drama, and no sense of panic until the moment of his delivery.

Paul often speaks of watching Dr. Thompson draw a line across my belly, just below my navel, with what looked like a Sharpie marker. He watched as the scalpel cut into my skin. He stood, as if in a tunnel, a vacuum with no sound, as he watched Dr. Thompson extract Joshua from my womb. Because he could see, he's the one who remembers that Joshua's head was turned to the right, resting on his right shoulder. His mouth was wide open, and he was trying with all his might to cry, but not a sound escaped his lips. His arms were skinny and wrinkled. His right arm was laid back with his right hand in a little fist. He was so tiny, so skinny. His color was dark and blotchy, almost purple.

"Floppy" is the word doctors use to describe babies born like Joshua. He scored a zero on his Apgar test. My mother was avoiding my eyes. I knew that something was severely wrong. The nurse took him to the counter where two additional nurses awaited to assist. There was a warming light above the counter. One of the nurses picked up the phone, dialed, spoke a few words into the receiver and hung up. Within minutes, the room was full of doctors and nurses. They said nothing to me, and they swept Joshua out. I kept asking, "Why can't I hear my baby cry?", and "Is he okay?"

Eventually Paul said, "Yes, honey, he's okay. He's just having a little problem crying. They're cleaning him up."

Dr. Thompson said, "We need to get you stitched up and into recovery."

I was in my recovery room with Paul and my mother by my side when Dr. Thompson came to see me. She said, "We have terrible news. We're not exactly sure what's going on with Joshua, but he has some sort of disorder, and we do not think he will survive the day."

My reaction was instinctual and guttural as a scream found its way out from the depths of my soul. I screamed at the top of my lungs and was immediately given a sedative. Sobbing, I turned to my mom and asked, "What sin did I commit that I would have brought this to my child?"

Like an experienced yachtsman who navigates waterways with their inner compass, my mother's unwavering faith gently rose to the surface as she answered, "Alison, I'm thinking of John 9, that God's glory will be revealed through this child." Right after she spoke those words, the sedative kicked in, and while the next few hours are foggy, I was still aware that this nightmare was actually reality.

Dr. Thompson cancelled the rest of her day and stayed with me. It was imperative to her that I had the chance to meet my baby, and so going against hospital protocol, she ordered a wheelchair for me and brought me down the hall to the NICU (Neonatal Intensive Care Unit). Sitting in the wheelchair, a wall of plastic separating me from my son, by then several hours old and covered in wires attached to life support, on a ventilator, I reached two fingers through the holes on the side of his NICU crib to touch Joshua for the first time. Everything faded into the distance. I didn't see his frailty, the wires, or the other incubators in the NICU. I only saw my little boy, and I was hopelessly in love.

Forty-eight hours into this ordeal, I felt as if I was coming out of a fog. I'd stopped taking pain medicine because I sensed its presence in my milk was making Josh lethargic. It was then, as if on cue, my fight or flight instinct kicked in. I was a scrappy kid from Long Island, born the only girl and youngest of five children, and this was my son's life at stake. "Flight" was not in my vocabulary. I remember, with perfect clarity, the moment that instinct kicked in. Dr. Wright, a cardiologist monitoring Joshua, came in to tell us that one of Joshua's heart valves had been leaking, but overnight had repaired itself. It ignited a spark in me. Deep down I knew, without a doubt, that God had Joshua in the palm of his hand, and if that was the case, then this was a battle worth every ounce of effort I had.

Hours after the doctor told us about Joshua's heart, I sat next to him in the NICU. I'd only been a mother for a short time, but I was about to add a new title to my identity. I looked at the nurse and said, "Let's give him a chance to live. Let's see what he can do if we take him off oxygen." That moment, and those words, changed everything. Right then and there, I became his advocate, fighting for the life of my son. That was the first time, but certainly not the last, that Joshua would breathe on his own when modern medicine said that he shouldn't. For years to come, I would find

13

myself staring death in the face and saying, "Let's give him a chance to live." And time and time again, Joshua would live.

Those days spent in the NICU are etched into the walls of my heart, but memory is a tricky thing. Some memories are as clear as the day they became a part of my story. Day after day, I would spend hours beside my little guy, hooked up to countless machines. Then, I would go home night after night to an empty bassinet in my bedroom. The bassinet was handed down through my family and shared with twenty-six babies. It was carefully restored for my son and placed with immense excitement in my bedroom as I anxiously awaited his arrival. I'm sure you can imagine how impossible it is for any mother to forget the agony of those nights. On the other hand, I was running on adrenaline and protected by shock. Days ran into each other, and facts about life happening outside the hospital became irrelevant. Nothing mattered but my son. My life became a marathon. With each glimmer of hope, another distance marker was reached. I studied every facet of my son's face, determined to memorize every line. He had the biggest eyes you've ever seen. We talked every day, all day. I would whisper promises of the life he'd live once we got out of there, and he would talk to me through his eyes, telling me how to fight for him.

Joshua's doctors were searching high and low for a diagnosis. We knew that having a diagnosis would help put us on a path toward treatment. With every test result that came back, the neo-natal team would report the results and tell us, "The test came back negative. Keep praying." But, after 24 days of testing and meetings with geneticists, talks of muscle and nerve biopsies, meetings with heart and other medical specialists, our baby remained undiagnosed.

The doctors would not release Joshua until we learned to put the feeding tube down his nose and into his stomach rather than his esophagus. I cried through my first attempt. Once we mastered that skill, we were ready to take our son home.

"There's nothing more we can do for you," we were told. "If your son is alive in a year, bring him back and we'll re-evaluate him." Those words penetrated my heart and left me in despair. They created cycles of depression as they echoed in my ear for the next eleven months.

14

We went home in a daze, without any directions, therapies, or ways to care for our son. We were not told what to do if he had a mucous plug, or how to revive him if he stopped breathing. We had no equipment other than a suction machine and an apnea monitor which would go off if his heart stopped. It was obvious the doctors were sending us home to care for a baby they did not think would make it more than a few days. The doctors were not at fault in their discharge orders as there truly was no protocol. There truly was no hope, medically speaking, that is.

For us, this amazing journey was just beginning.

CHAPTER 4

CHAOS IN THE MIDST OF LIFE
Alison

Many of those early days, we were like the majority of new parents. Learning the new rhythm of life, working through our new identities as parents, falling in love with our son—those aspects, I'm sure, are universal. Other aspects, however, were entirely different. Throughout the years I've heard countless moms mention their fear as they drove away from the hospital, wondering how they were supposed to keep their kid alive. What they were trying to say is that this new reality still feels very foreign. For me, the fear was literal. At any point, my son could die.

It was now up to us to learn the ins and outs of taking care of a newborn with a life-threatening disorder. Not only did we have to learn all of Joshua's distress signals, but we also had to learn basic daily tasks, like how to feed him. I cried as I installed that feeding tube, but I did it, repeatedly, until it became my new *normal*. The first few weeks that Joshua was home, Paul and I worked side by side learning how to be the very best parents we could, and more importantly, figuring out how to keep our son alive. But for what it was, the honeymoon wouldn't last long.

On February 15, two weeks after Josh was born and nine days before he was released from the hospital, Paul was chosen in the expansion team draft as the Jacksonville Jaguars 9th pick. At the time, the NFL was just beginning to shift toward a Monday through Friday team workout during the off-season. The NY Jets hadn't yet adopted the new schedule, and we planned for him to train at home in Dallas during the off season. But, because it was the first season for the Jaguars and therefore Tom Coughlin's first year with his new team, Tom called for strict Monday through Friday workouts. Life in the NFL doesn't stop because your son was born with a life-threatening disorder, and Paul's attendance was what they call in the NFL "voluntary/mandatory."

By the beginning of March, mere weeks after bringing Josh home, Paul began his weekly commute to Jacksonville, Florida. Every Sunday afternoon Joshua and I would kiss him goodbye, and every Friday evening he would race home from the airport, eager to spend thirty-six hours by his son's bedside. We spent a ton of money on airfare those first few years. Over the weekend, Paul would assume the role of caregiver, which provided me space for a much-needed break. Monday through Friday I lived in a constant state of fight or flight, and those thirty-six hours gave me just enough rest to be able to do it again the next week.

In June, while on a break from training and taking a needed family vacation in Maine, we received a packet in the mail. It was a four-page printout from a medical article about Myotubular Myopathy (MTM). Earlier in the spring, mom and I had taken Josh to the Scottish Rite Hospital for a muscle biopsy, and this package contained the reports that revealed the results. One of the articles in the package was published in 1967, and we were introduced to phrases like these quotes from a medical journal:

"Centronuclear myopathy is a group of pathologically defined disorders that characteristically have a high proportion of small myofibers with centrally placed nuclei."

"Spiro, et al. first described the term 'myotubular myopathy' in 1967."

"X-linked myotubular myopathy (XLMTM) is a rare congenital muscle disorder."

"Male infants present severe hypotonia, and generalized muscle weakness, and the disorder is most often complicated by respiratory failure."

The articles even included apparent death sentences such as, "Approximately 75% of severely affected neonates die within the first few weeks of months of life due to respiratory insufficiency," and "The average life expectancy of XLMTM patients is 29 months."

The news was dismal and there was no upside and no hope given from the medical community. Joshua's muscles were desperately weak. There was no ongoing research and no cure. What little hope we could conjure up came from deep within ourselves.

But Joshua finally had a diagnosis. It was diagnosis so rare that at the time only fifty-five people worldwide shared it. But at last, his disorder finally had a name! While it was comforting to finally have a diagnosis, it seemed as if every single aspect of caring for a child with MTM could only be learned through on-the-job training.

Mercifully, Paul and I were together when Joshua got pneumonia as we were packing to go home at the end of the month. Instead of flying back to Dallas, we checked Joshua into the local hospital and ourselves into the nearest hotel. Our traveling nurse we'd brought with us provided a tremendous amount of help over the next seven days. We traded day/night shifts at the hospital and ventured into our first real experience of telling doctors how to care for our son. Joshua fought through the illness, and we headed back to Dallas just in time for Paul to catch a plane to the Jaguars' training camp in Wisconsin.

The first week of August, three weeks into training camp, Joshua had his first mucous plug. This sounds quite manageable, but the event introduced us to the fact that Joshua was more fragile than we'd ever imagined. A mucous plug obstructing his airway gave us seconds to respond and clear his airway, or we'd be thrown into a life-or-death situation. The house flew into crisis mode as my mother and I raced to save Joshua's life. Life-flight arrived and landed in our quiet cul-de-sac. I'm quite certain the whirling of helicopter propellers right outside their front door was a first for the neighbors in our upper middle class suburban neighborhood.

Paul was in the players dorms at Stevens Point, Wisconsin when that first phone call came. How he managed to keep it together while he played, I'll never know. But I do know that it wreaked havoc on his emotions. That night, robbed of any way to help us, he paced the halls of the dorm. Up and down, he walked, pacing and praying, begging God to spare his son's life, while I hovered over Joshua's hospital bed, 1,300 miles away, begging my son to stay with me. I can only imagine the feelings of helplessness Paul must have struggled with. In my mind, it feels like a cold, wild-eyed panic.

The kind of panic that feels claustrophobic, as if the world is closing in around you.

Toward the end of that August, after we got back from the hospital and after six months of living on the brink of complete exhaustion, my mom had to go to New York to close her father's estate. This left me completely housebound from 8 a.m. when the nurse left until 10 p.m. when she came back. At 10 p.m., I would run to the grocery store to grab a few things before they closed and then rush back home to catch a few hours of sleep as time allowed. A few weeks into this new routine and I was on the brink of a nervous breakdown. Every human has a breaking point, and by mid-September, I reached mine.

To complicate the situation, I also had to pack our Dallas home because football season was quickly approaching in Jacksonville. To an outsider, this might sound crazy, but I was still an NFL wife, and there are expectations. My mom flew back to Dallas to help me as I finished last minute preparations, which included shipping half our belongings cross-country. This would be our first move with Joshua, and we would do it semi-annually for the next two years, spending the off season in Dallas and the football season in Florida.

I've lost count of how many phone calls Paul received those first few years, letting him know we were in crisis mode and that Joshua was in a literal fight for his life. This was before every person walking down the sidewalk had a cell phone. I called the front desk at the Jaguars office and told the secretary, "This is Alison Frase and I need to talk to Paul immediately. It's Joshua."

Everybody associated with the Jaguars at the time knew who we were and how bad it was, so they flew into action. Once, Paul was on the tarmac in Tampa after a game against the Buccaneers. Their plane was delayed due to maintenance issues. Joshua was eight months old and had contracted Respiratory Syncytial Virus (RSV)—a virus that can be fatal for healthy children, and we were rushing to the hospital.

Wayne Weaver, the original owner of the Jaguars, had his assistant searching for a commercial flight that Paul could get on to get back to Jacksonville as quickly as possible. But, as it was 11 p.m., there were no flights available. Paul's teammates were chattering around him, some listening to their music, some trying to catch some sleep, while Paul sat there, his body motionless and his mind racing. If the plane could ever get off the ground, Paul would only be an hour away from home. But, when your son is teetering on the brink of death, that hour can stretch out toward eternity. Sometime around four in the morning, hours after their scheduled arrival, the team pulled in on a bus, and before heading to the stadium to let the players go home, they stopped at the hospital to let Paul get to his family. It was the longest bus ride of his life.

I remember one morning I woke up with this gut instinct, my compass that I relied on throughout Joshua's life and at every crossroad, and I knew I had a significant decision to make. I looked at Paul and said, "I'm going to start a foundation, a nonprofit, and I'm going to use your NFL connections and our Wall Street friends. I will not sit by and watch our son become another statistic." Paul replied that he'd been talking with his teammate Pat Kelly who had moved on to Wall Street after his NFL career. Pat and he were talking about raising some money for research. This was no coincidence. This was the birth of our son's foundation, The Joshua Frase Foundation for Congenital Myopathy Research, Inc. I received a download and full scope of the vision later.

While Paul grappled with the rigors of making a team in the NFL, and then performing well enough to keep his position, I was wrestling with the paperwork and logistics while forming a 501C3 non-profit organization to help our son. We were motivated to find answers and we had the resolve necessary to carry out the vision of a better future for our Joshua.

A month later, we filed the founding paperwork for the Joshua Frase Foundation. MTM was so rare that there was virtually no ongoing research in the US. Paul and I decided we had to do whatever we could to raise awareness for this disorder and raise money to fund research. Orphan diseases, maladies that affect less than 200,000 people worldwide, don't get financial attention unless they affect someone in the limelight, and the NFL offered us that light and a huge platform to bring MTM to the forefront of the minds of some of our friends in high places.

The following spring, after we'd returned to Dallas and Paul had already begun his weekly commute to Jacksonville, my mother and I were headed to an appointment for Joshua. We were constantly looking for any type of intervention, whether through the traditional medicine route or a more alternative form of medicine. I searched high and low for help. That day, we were on I-635 in gridlock traffic. Joshua began vomiting in the backseat and quickly entered respiratory distress mode. I jerked the car over to the side of the road and hopped out, desperate to get him out of the backseat so that I could clear his airway. The tube for the suction machine was clogged because of the excessive amounts of mucous coming from his lungs. Coincidentally, a nurse pulled up alongside us and asked me if I needed something. I frantically asked her if she had any liquid in her car, and in response, she handed me a can of Coke. I used the machine to suck the Coke up through the suction catheter and managed to dislodge the mucous blocking the tube, and then I continued to work on Joshua. We were still on the side of the road, and by that time, a semi-truck driver noticed our precarious situation. He asked what I needed, and I told him I needed to get off at the next exit. To my utter amazement, he pulled his rig through that gridlocked traffic and turned it so that it completely blocked traffic, while I raced in my car up the shoulder of the road and then off the exit.

We got to Medical City where we sat in the parking lot, working on Joshua for an hour. As strange as it seems, I knew in my gut that I needed to avoid a hospital stay if possible. After an hour of intense work, Joshua returned to normal, and we all got back in the car and drove home where I called Paul to let him know about the bizarre afternoon we'd just had.

As hard as it was for Paul to be away from us much of the time and as hard as it was for me to be the primary caregiver for Josh, it was necessary. The NFL has excellent benefits, including carte blanch insurance. The problem was that no insurance company knew how to properly support the demands of a child with MTM. It wasn't just the insurance company; we didn't know what we needed either. From the beginning, they provided a night nurse from 10 p.m. to 8 a.m. so that my mother and I could get a good night's sleep. It took a year and a half for us to get a pulse oximeter, the device that told me Joshua's heart rate and oxygen levels. Before that, I judged everything by the color of his skin. Pink skin and bright eyes meant we were doing okay. In a second, his bright eyes could communicate distress. My eyes would shift to his chest as I registered the rhythm of his

21

breathing, and then instantly, I looked at his skin. Pink healthy skin would shift to dull gray with blue undertones. Mucous plugs were almost always the suspect, but a collapsed lung or pneumonia could turn his skin deadly blue.

I spent hours those first few years, calling other MTM moms and asking what their insurance company did for them. Then I called the director of team benefits for the NFL asking for the next piece of equipment to help in Joshua's care and additional nursing hours.

Time went on, and my mother and I became quite a team. While my mother performed basic tasks for Joshua, I was the one who pulled the bulk of his care. My mom, meanwhile, took care of me. There would be days when the weight of MTM seemed too heavy to carry, and I felt my shoulders crumbling under the constant pressure to keep my son alive. My mother could sense it, she could see it in my eyes the same way I could see distress in Joshua's eyes, and she would make me some tea. As she handed me the tea, she'd say, "Here sweetie, drink this. I know this is the hardest battle you've ever had to face. My heart breaks for you, but you can't stay here too long. You must get back up and push on, for Joshua." I can't tell you how many times she poured me a cup of tea, but I can tell you she poured her strength into me, and in turn, I could do the same for my son.

I remember those few years as a series of moves. We moved in and out of hospital stays. We moved back and forth from Jacksonville. Eventually, in the summer of 1997, convinced that Paul was going to be with the Jaguars for the foreseeable future, and equally convinced that I could no longer go on without him home, we put our house on the market in Dallas and began looking for a house in Atlantic Beach, Florida. It only took a little bit of searching before we found a house at the beach that we loved. After a quick closing, we began renovations. Paul did what he could while he was in town, and once he started training camp, I took over. Meanwhile, I finalized the closing on our Dallas home, overseeing the renovations of our new home and working on the Foundation—which was just beginning to gain momentum.

At the end of August, the day before the final cut deadline, Josh had a rough week and Paul told Coach Coughlin that he was headed back to Dallas for the weekend. Tom told him to be back by Tuesday, and Paul said he would. Fifteen minutes after Paul walked through our Dallas doorway, the phone rang. I answered it, and my heart sunk when I heard Tom's voice on the other end. Head coaches never call their players. He'd been traded to the Packers and was expected to report immediately. I looked up at him and said, "I'll see you in Jacksonville when the season is over." My decision to skip out on that football season was immediate and firm.

Paul and I knew the chaos of the life of an NFL journeyman. It was a great disappointment to be forced to leave what Paul had been a part of starting in Jacksonville, but the fact was, Paul still had a job. He had not been cut but traded, and to a team that had just won the Super Bowl. And we still had insurance benefits.

He flew out the next morning to Green Bay, Wisconsin with two pairs of pants, two shirts, and a pair of shoes in his suitcase. I began packing everything we owned into 190 boxes in preparation for the movers who were coming to take them to Florida.

Medical Journal Referenced:

Jeon JH, Namgung R, Park MS, et al. X-linked myotubular myopathy in a family with two infant siblings: a case with MTM1 mutation. *Yonsei Med J*. 2011;52(3):547-550. doi:10.3349/ymj.2011.52.3.547
https://www.ncbi.nlm.nih.gov/pmc/articles/PMC3101044/

CHAPTER 5

THE YEARS: THEY CHANGED ME
Alison

I was thirty-one when Josh was born. I'd spent the previous decade climbing toward success. My career had taken the exact path I'd hoped for. I left it all to follow my soon–to–be–husband in his career, a decision made less out of tradition and more as a result of my new role as an NFL wife. We gallivanted around the globe—footloose and fancy free—until the day I found myself on an operating table at Medical City in Dallas, TX.

Change, for me, happened in two ways. It was sudden; shattering dreams into 1,000 tiny pieces of glass around my feet. The shards of my shattered dreams cut deep as I walked past the empty family bassinet in my room. And it was gradual, shifting the fabric of who I was as I aligned my core with the reality of my life.

I drifted in and out of that acceptance for the first eighteen months of Joshua's life. "This is my new reality," my heart whispered, and I felt my shoulders sag under the weight that came with that knowledge. I could handle the truth at home, but if I took Josh into public… one wayward stare from a child or one mom shielding their child in hopes they wouldn't *catch* my son's disease, and I ran home in tears, defeated.

Stronger than defeat was shame. Some friends fell by the wayside because they didn't know what to say, or it was just too much for them. Strangers looked at my son with disgust, and I knew it was because of me. I was a Rockett. I'd grown up under a roof where one of our daily mottos was, "Good, better, best—never let it rest—'til the good is better and the better is best." We were raised to be overachievers at our core, and I'd succeeded at what I thought was one of life's greatest failures.

I'd given my son the disorder that the doctors said would take his life.

It was because of me. I carried the gene. Strangers were looking at my son, but their disgust was for me. They might not have known it, but I did, and I crumpled under the weight of my failure even as I sang lullabies to my son at night.

The first eighteen months felt like an earthquake ripping through the fabric of my life, leaving me raw and exposed. I moved through my days living between extremes: I was alone, but I had a handful of trustworthy, earnest people I could lean on. They were true friends. The doctors couldn't help, but I had a God-given instinct when it came to my son's needs. I blamed myself for giving him this disorder, but everything fell by the wayside when we were laying on the living room floor laughing at something we saw on TV.

I knew my son could die without a moment's notice, but he was alive right then, and I had to choose him over the fear.

Those early days were a struggle, but they were also a gift. Joshua, my faithful guide, was teaching me how to fight for him. A tool not of my choosing was refining me, and those days laid a foundation for how we would walk through this journey.

I slowly rose above the shame and the fear and accepted the cards I was dealt. I didn't understand the purpose, and I sometimes fell prey to the guilt my DNA would lay on me, but the pure honest truth was that Joshua exemplified love. He exemplified unconditional love, and his love was changing me from the inside out.

CHAPTER 6

PERCEPTIONS CHANGE IN QUEBEC
Paul

Alison and I were very blessed to have a support system like her mom and the wonderful nurses to fall back on. Elsie sacrificed her life, putting it on hold for over three years, to help us with Joshua.

We were burnt out and in desperate need of a reprieve. Previously, our bucket list included traveling to Europe, but we knew that was out of the question. We could not leave for more than a few days, and we never went anywhere far from home for fear of the unimaginable happening and our inability to return home on the drop of a dime. We had heard that Quebec City in Canada was considered a "little Europe" of sorts with the flare of the European architecture and culture. We decided to go to old Quebec City for a couple of days and then spend a couple more days in the countryside along the St. Lawrence River. Elsie would stay behind and hold down the fort with our nurses.

We were always apprehensive about leaving Joshua, but we were in such need of a break that we planned the trip and left a couple of weeks later. We landed in Canada and had a couple of hours to drive. Elsie had told us of a Catholic church that was well known as a place of respite and healing. It was the Basilica of Ste Anne de Beaupre which Elsie had visited when she was eighteen years old while on a trip with some relatives. She remembered walking into the cathedral and seeing many crutches and old wheelchairs hanging from the walls. There were stories of miraculous healings that had taken place in this church. We were going to stop there and say a prayer for our son.

Before we reached the cathedral, we passed the Montmorency Falls. This waterfall is one and a half times the height of Niagara Falls and is located along the St. Lawrence River. We stopped at the park and climbed to a platform located off the side of the falls. A thick cloud of mist rose off the bottom of the falls, created by the spray of the water slamming against the rocks. It was a cloudy day, and I imagined the rainbow a sunny day would have created as the sun shone through the mist. The mist was cool on our faces. There was a little chill in the air, which was to be expected on a cloudy day in Canada, even in the summertime.

We left the falls and started toward the basilica that Alison's mom and dad had visited almost half of a century before. We drove through the Canadian countryside, admiring the beautiful landscape. There were areas of thick forests that would suddenly open to rolling pastures and fields of grass stretching for miles. There were areas of steep, mountainous inclines with sheer rock cliffs and other areas of flat farmland where we could see cattle and livestock grazing in the distance.

We came upon the city of Ste Anne de Beaupre and followed the signs to the famous Basilica. As we approached, we were reminded of the incredible architecture of cathedrals across the northeastern landscape of the United States. The steeples that protruded through the tops of the trees in this tiny Quebec town, reminded us of St. Patrick's Cathedral of New York City. St. Patrick's was an incredible replica of some of the basilicas built in Europe. The basilica of St. Anne De Beaupre had evolved over the years into one of the most beautiful basilicas in Canada and is known for the pilgrimages that began in the mid-1600s. We fell silent as we pulled into the parking lot, transfixed by the beauty that stood before us.

As we entered St. Anne's Cathedral, a wave of peace seemed to pass over us. We were in awe at the sight of hundreds of sets of crutches hanging from the ceiling and walls. Old, empty wheelchairs with thin, worn wheels and rusted frames lined the walls. Some of the crutches were very worn. I remember old, tattered pieces of cloth wrapped around the handles of the crutches, obviously to protect the user from getting blisters on their hands as they walked countless steps while on their pilgrimage to St. Anne's.

Alison and I knelt and prayed a prayer of healing for our son. We sat and enjoyed a moment of quietness together. Neither of us needed to speak. We just watched people come and go while we prayed for our Josh and reflected on our journey. I later learned that over 1.5 million people per year visit the Basilica of St. Anne de Beaupre for a myriad of reasons. I believe it's a place where God meets the hearts of His people. We left that place of worship with a sense of being closer to our Maker. Just the thought of the millions of people over the previous 400 years that had visited and worshiped at St. Anne's astounded us. Now we could say, as could Elsie, that we had completed our pilgrimage. Ours had ended with a prayer and petition to God for the life of our son. We had stood in the gap for him, and we chose life over death, hope over despair, and light over darkness. The struggle was only beginning.

The next couple of days we spent in Old Quebec where we thoroughly enjoyed walking the streets of the old walled heart of Quebec City. We eventually found ourselves in a section of town where a flea market was staged. The narrow cobblestone alleys were lined with local artisans exhibiting their wares and talents on the canvas. We stopped to talk to one of the artists while we admired her work. We even bought a couple of pen and ink renditions of the Chateau Frontenac and the Holy Trinity Anglican Cathedral, other famous landmarks located in Old Quebec.

As we were walking amongst the little booths down those alleys, we saw a family walking through the flea market that caught our eye. The father, who was pushing a stroller with his son in it, looked tired. The mother, a step behind, was forcing herself to keep up. She had a look on her face as if she would like to disappear into one of the artist's paintings of serenity and leave this world and all its heartache and troubles behind. I thought I could detect shame and anguish on her face. I could sense Alison beginning to get emotional and I saw her eyes tear up. She knelt down next to the stroller and took the little boy's hand in hers and began to talk to the child. The child clearly had a severe muscle disorder. He was listless and could not respond. The family we were looking at was a mirror image of Alison, Josh, and I just a year and a half before.

Alison leaned over and gave the little boy a kiss, stood up, gravitated toward the mother, and began talking softly. I knelt down and put my hand on the boy's shoulder and told him it was nice to meet him. I stood and asked the father how he was doing, and I told him briefly about our Josh. Their story was not unlike ours. The disorder was X-linked—mother is the carrier of the gene—and the mother took a lot of guilt and shame on herself. He told me that his wife didn't even want to be out in public, but he was going to get his family out and try to have as normal of a life as possible. Meanwhile, Alison was encouraging the mom and giving her hope. She encouraged her to focus on their child and to embrace the gift that God had given them.

Our happenstance meeting came to an end and we went our separate ways. Alison and I hoped that we lifted the spirits of that mom and dad. You see, two years prior, before Joshua was born, that conversation would have never taken place. It wouldn't have taken place because we would have stayed in our spot on the other side of the street. Our hearts would've ached for that family, but we never would have made contact and encouraged them. It was reinforced that day: our perception had changed and our actions reflected our new perceptions.

More importantly though, that conversation highlighted the change I'd witnessed in Alison. She was different now. Stronger. More confident in herself and the new direction her life was headed in. She was keenly aware that life was hard, but it was also beautiful. I watched her choose beauty time and time again. I loved watching her offer that lonely mother support that day. Joshua was changing her. He was changing us. He was making us better.

CHAPTER 7

A VISION OF HOPE

Alison

I love this scripture:

For the vision is yet for an appointed time, but at the end it shall speak, and not lie: though it tarry, wait for it; because it will surely come, it will not tarry. Habakkuk 2:3. King James Version

The foundation, like my son, was two years old, and we knew that we needed to fund cutting-edge research. At the time, very little research was currently funded here in the US. Finding the right research, at the right time, and with the right team was a daunting task.

The only way I know to describe this to you is with a picture. Imagine a lab mouse in search of food. He's never been in this particular maze before, but experience has taught him that food is behind one of the doors. The maze itself is nothing more than a long line of doors, one after the other, and there's a little button he can push to get the door to open. The mouse, we'll call him Miles, goes from door to door. Sniffing. Searching. Desperate for food. He opens door after door to no avail. Miles was right, there was food—but it was tucked away in a corner of the maze where trails hadn't been placed yet.

That's where Paul and I were during Joshua's first year. There were no answers. There were no care guidelines. There was no research. And there were no doctors who knew what they were looking at when they viewed his file. We were knocking on every door, but to no avail. I knew that there had to be an answer though, or at least I hoped that there might be. The life of my son hung in the balance. It just made sense to me that if we couldn't find the right trail, then we needed to make one.

It's hard for me tell this part of my story without talking about my faith. The beginning of the foundation, from my point of view, is so interwoven with my faith that I don't know where one begins and the other ends. We started the foundation with the mission to raise money to fund cutting-edge research, and we relied on Paul's platform in the NFL and my New York chutzpah—Paul's description ☺. But to be honest, we didn't know which direction we should head in regarding the science.

My mother and I were in our beach house in Atlantic Beach while Paul was off playing for the Green Bay Packers in the season of 1997. Mom was watching CNN and the special spotlighted regenerative medicine research. On the spot, she decided to call the physician highlighted, Dr. Anthony Atala.

At that time, Dr. Atala was at Boston Children's Hospital and Harvard Medical School. His area of focus was regenerative medicine, stem cell, specifically urology, and he was successfully growing a human bladder outside of the body in a cell culture dish—in vitro. Much to our surprise, Dr. Atala returned my mother's call and the three of us spoke at length. I shared about Joshua, the inception of the Foundation before Joshua's first birthday, and the direction we felt needed to be taken. As the conversation progressed, my mom shared her heart and how she'd felt very strongly from the day of Joshua's birth that, "We are not sure why this has happened to Paul and Alison, but I believe God has a plan in all of this."

Dr. Atala's reply was "Amen." I will remember his "Amen" for the rest of my life. He said he would speak with some of his colleagues and see if there was a way he might be able to help.

Dr. Atala promised to get back to us "in several weeks." The instant I hung up the phone, I had a vision. It became my seed of hope.

In the vision, I saw myself handing Dr. Atala a check. I saw his face, I shook his hand, and an agreement was made. I said, "Mom, I'm not sure how to interpret this," and I shared with her what had just happened.

She paused and responded. "If you feel that was truly from God then I will believe and stand with you, Honey." It was then, at that moment, a seed of hope was planted deep within my heart. It was a seed that would grow until it became a powerful force in my life. I learned over time that hope could endure almost anything. It became my fuel. Hope allowed me to persevere in situations where all seemed lost.

Perhaps some would say hope was my escape, that I was denying the facts and not in touch with reality. Maybe they would say that I was in denial and unable to face the fact that my son was born with a death sentence. A death sentence so tangible that each and every day of his existence was a sheer miracle. But, I say, hope became my drive.

When I looked at my son, I did not see his twisted frail body, I saw his eyes—beautiful, piercing green eyes that held a depth of understanding far beyond his young life. I could get lost in his eyes. When I couldn't understand his audible voice, I could look in his eyes and there was a connection so deep that I could read his every need. His eyes opened my heart to an understanding of life much deeper and much greater than I had ever known. I saw hope in my son's eyes.

Dr. Henry Cloud, who is an acclaimed leadership expert, psychologist, and best-selling author, stated that, "Hope is about always holding on when it looks bad and being able to hold on, sometimes for a long time." Dr. Cloud also informed us that the time dimension is a key component, and if it did not require time, we would have no purpose for hope. But for us, that time dimension was inseparable from the reality that our son was fighting a clock from the moment he entered this world. It was a constant battle wedged between living in the realm of hope while being stuck in the physical state, which was the reality of the frailty of our son. I was constantly balancing hope, faith, reality, a vision, and the wisdom to hear God's voice at those crossroads of Joshua's care, our family, and the foundation.

Our hope against hope was clinging to a mere possibility that something good would take place, and is it not our human nature to find fresh cause for optimism? Hope is all we had and in desperation, we hung on for our dear son's life.

CHAPTER 8

JFF: IT WAS TIME TO FLEX OUR MUSCLES
Paul

After we settled into a routine of survival, I began to reach out to Pat Kelly, my best man at our wedding. Shortly after Joshua's birth he reached out to see how the three of us were faring. During the call, he made me promise not to lose touch, as he wanted to help any way he could.

We were teammates at Syracuse, and he'd been drafted in the 7th round of the 1988 draft to the Denver Broncos. He ended up the #2 tight end that year backing up Orson Mobley. Unfortunately, Pat blew out the anterior cruciate ligament (ACL) in his knee toward the end of the second quarter of the AFC Championship game, which sidelined him for the Super Bowl two weeks later. The Jets liked his size and ability and took Pat in a trade with the Broncos at the close of his second year, making us teammates once again.

Pat was the team genius in college. Brilliant and hilarious, he was the go-to-guy for solutions to all kinds of predicaments his teammates, me included, found themselves in from time to time. It's unusual that the comic relief is also the sensible problem solver who held a respectable GPA, but Pat had the combination down. We loved and envied him at the same time. Whether we wished we were as funny, smart, or as much of a babe magnet as Pat, we all wanted a piece of him.

About the same time that Alison and her mom began to reach out to Dr. Atala at Boston Children's Hospital, my discussions with Pat turned to fundraising opportunities. When Pat retired from the NFL a few years before, he'd joined Behr Stearns as an investment banker, and true to form, he'd climbed the corporate ladder and had achieved what very few are able to do in such a short amount of time in the industry. Pat had risen in the ranks of the Manhattan home base of Behr, and they had promoted him to a position in Boston, heading up an entire group in that office. He was climbing to high places. But more importantly for this immediate need, he'd gained the admiration of his mentors who were some of the most influential and wealthy men and women in the financial markets. And, lucky for us, they were eager to get behind great causes that would make a difference in humanity at some level.

Pat said, "Paul, it's time we started fundraising for this. Let's throw a big party here in Boston and we'll get our Syracuse alumni together as well as some heavy hitters I'm working with and raise a bunch of money." I told Pat this was a confirmation as Alison and her mother were making inroads with some of the brightest scientists in the world located practically in Pat's backyard, and we knew it would take money to push research forward. How much money? We had no idea, but we had to start somewhere and spur these scientists into action for the cause of MTM. At that time, the industry was starting to scream about how expensive it was to develop and produce a small molecule pharmaceutical. We didn't look at the billion-dollar mark as a goal, but when it came to our child, there wasn't a number that would stop us from trying to find a cure. We didn't have answers, or even a true direction, but we did have deep connections within the NFL, as well as some important ties to the financial markets through Pat. It was time to start making some noise, as if our son's life depended on it.

CHAPTER 9

THE GALA
Alison

In 1997, the Hard Rock Café in Boston, Massachusetts was situated in the Copley Square area. At night, its neon lights could be seen blocks away. We rented out the whole restaurant for the event, moving tables out of the way to create space for the massive cocktail party that was about to happen. Our auction items were complemented by the Hard Rock Café's classic decorating style of music memorabilia layered on the walls throughout the restaurant. I partnered with the Muscular Dystrophy Association (MDA) for our first gala, and we were bringing in football alumni from around the country.

Excitement was pumping through my veins. As the night progressed, we filled the room with teammates and alumni from Syracuse, NFL teams Paul played on, a few music legends, and friends from Wall Street. We called them our Muscle Dream Team. I felt like I was doing something good for my son that night.

Two months prior, Paul had reached out to the MDA's regional Boston office and discovered a former classmate from Syracuse worked there. That gave us the "in" we were looking for to create the first event. The MDA has been at the forefront of raising large amounts of money for neuromuscular disorders since they became an organization in 1950. A couple of years after the first event, we were interviewed by Jerry Lee Lewis the year that MDA commenced streaming the telethon on the internet. Jerry opened the show by stating that it was the first year they were "live" streaming across the entire world wide web! We needed to use their logistical experience due to the challenges that had arisen from me living in Jacksonville and planning the first event in Boston. Their history in the city allowed them to elevate the event in a way that I could never have done as a stranger to the city.

In addition to working with the local MDA representative, I set my sights at the executive level. In the same way that I needed their access to local businesses, I knew they were eager to gain access to our contacts in the NFL. I also knew that to get our newly established research team at Harvard any funding from this event, I would have to negotiate an agreement with the Director of Research and also the president of the association. We spent two months hashing out the details, and three days prior to the event I threatened to pull our list of contacts off the table unless they gave me what I asked for: dollar for dollar, our researchers would receive what we raised the night of the event.

We raised $144,000 that night.

Our event became known as the JFF Muscle Dream Team Gala, and it grew to be one of the top five social events in Boston. I changed the theme every year, but the one thing that kept us unique was that I kept the feel of a mix and mingle four-hour cocktail party. Tickets to our gala sold for $1,500, and we sold out. Each event built upon the previous year, and we continued to secure bigger and better venues, entertainment, food, and auction items. It was a challenge for me to make them better every year, but I loved and thrived on that challenge! Our events sold out for twelve years in a row.

Speaking of auction items, ours were outrageous! They ranged from a signed Beatles travel bag owned by one of the Beatles and signed by all four, an Elvis Presley signed guitar that I bought for $5,000 and sold for $83,000, a Harley Davidson Road King I bought and added a custom paint job, making $15,000 (one of the hedge fund guys bought it, added a Raptor to it and gave it to his business partner as a gift). We sold dinner nights with private chefs in your home for $40,000, and two tickets to all four of the golf *major* tournaments for the year for anywhere from $15,000 - $28,000. We sold those for four consecutive years. Every year we had vacation packages to exclusive resorts around the world; some years we had tickets

36

to the US Open packaged with resort and airline tickets. One year we had tickets to runway shows during Fashion Week, and the winner could choose between Paris and New York.

The caliber of donors progressed dramatically, and the auction gave donors wanted exposure in our marketing campaign around the city. We had a two-story banner that hung in the archway at Rowes Wharf, one of the premium real estate spots in all of Boston. Sponsors paid between $15,000 and $50,000 to get their logo on the banner. I can still see that banner in my head. It's the picture of Paul holding Joshua and they're face to face. Our logo is on top of the picture with our web address just below Paul's body. Joshua was larger than life on that banner. I would look at the frailty of his body and think about how much he was accomplishing just by being alive. I cried every time I saw our banner hanging over the archway.

In addition to exposure on the banner, I created the Book of Hope. Measuring ten inches across the top and thirteen inches long, it was the same size as the "W" magazine and just as heavy in your hands. Paul and I wrote an annual letter to our gala attendees, acknowledging our committee, our board, and our donors. Donors coveted prime marketing spots in the Book of Hope and knew that their spot in the book directly correlated to the amount of donation via auction item or straight sponsorship. Inside the front and back cover spots were reserved for $50,000 sponsorships.

In a world where everyone wants to be the top dog, this marketing strategy produced great results. We were able to draw celebrities like Joey Kramer from Aerosmith, Chad Smith from the Red Hot Chili Peppers, and Peter Wolf from J. Geils Band. Football players like Kurt Warner, Don McPherson, Ronnie Lott, Jesse Palmer, Tony Boselli, Jim Kelly, and Daryl Johnston added to the celebrity status of the party. Over the next ten years, we raised over $7 million from our annual gala. That number excludes the first $400,000 raised in 1997 and 1998 when the money ran through the MDA first.

Because of our gala, we were able to flood our research institutions with private funding, no strings attached. It allowed our researchers the freedom to explore unknown realms of science with one goal in mind: find a treatment or cure for MTM. To say the very least, we were working with scientists willing to work at the cutting edge of their respective fields, and because of that, they drew attention from much larger donors than us. In 2001, we were able to draw in an additional $5 million over five years from the NIH. It was the first federal funding outside of our private dollars and a massive step in the right direction.

The Gala was working. Funding research and pushing science gave us a fighting chance to save these kids' lives. It gave us the chance to save Joshua's life.

CHAPTER 10

SEARCHING FOR DINOSAURS
Paul

In this business of raising money and writing checks to advance research, Alison and I still yearned for normalcy. We knew we needed to give Joshua wonderful experiences and the best life had to offer. So along with desperately trying to save our son's life, we gave him all that we could to experience life. One of these experiences began in Florida. After 2 ½ days, and about 1600 miles, we arrived at Alison's relatives in Owls Head, Maine. Uncles, aunts, grandma, and cousins. Joshua was about six years old, and he was about to experience "normal."

We had made our way past Baltimore in eighteen hours and it was time for me to sleep a bit. I'd usually get drowsy at about five a.m. on these long trips and push it for another thirty minutes or so before I had to pull over and rest. That morning, I pulled into the truck parking area of the rest stop, found a nice spot, put the RV in park, and proceeded to roll my seat back to a reclined position. I'd driven nearly eighteen hours straight, with a few bathroom breaks and food stops through the Carolinas. I didn't eat much food on those stops, but I loaded up on coffee to rev me up for the next leg of the trip. The coffee became counter-productive, and toothpicks holding the eyelids open (hypothetically of course) would only prove that one could sleep with his bloodshot eyes wide open.

After about an hour and a half of good sound sleep, the passengers started to stir. A window shade opened, and sunlight splashed into the vehicle. The stream of bright light woke everyone. A good stretch and a walk to the public restrooms were just enough to get the body moving again. A stop at the counter to buy another twenty-four-ounce black coffee would give me the jolt to get the RV on the road again. We only had another seven hours or so to get to Massapequa. In Massapequa, we ate a quick lunch and picked up Elsie, Amanda, and Brielle before getting back on the road to head for Maine. As they all loaded up, I hollered back to Josh that we were in for the ride of our lives as it was myself, Joshua, and six women for the next eight hours, all the way to Maine. Nanna, Nurse Linda, Molly, Alison, Amanda, and Brielle.

After a quick stop in Long Island, while passing through a rather rural area of Connecticut, I was commissioned by the majority to find a place to stop and rest. It was uncharacteristic of me to bend to the masses, especially when driving a long distance with the destination still hours away. But for some reason, I felt a little exploratory venture was in order. I pulled off the highway and quickly realized we were in a very rural area. There were no gas stations or convenience stores around, only green, lush forests. I drove a few miles over very hilly terrain and saw a sign for a state park. I turned in and wound my way through the forest to the parking area. It turned out that this was a very small state park, and it was known for its hiking trails. The trail followed beside a stream, so everyone put on their bathing suits just in case there was a spot to cool off on this hot summer day. The girls all ran ahead and Joshua and I followed behind. The trail was flat but was laden with roots from the many pine trees that lined the path, so it was slow going for Josh and me. We heard the girls up ahead hooting and hollering and screaming that the water was freezing. Joshua and I rolled out of the thicket and found ourselves on a bluff overlooking the swimming hole that Alison, Amanda, Brielle, and Molly had plunged into.

Joshua was getting a bit tired of sitting up in his wheelchair, so I held him and sat on the ground. I soaked in the serenity and surreal feeling of the moment. It was such a peaceful setting, sitting amongst the trees, watching the girls frolic in the water. The crystal-clear stream flowed with calmness as the breeze rustled the pine branches. We probably sat there for a good twenty minutes while Nanna and Linda made their way through the pine grove to join us. We all enjoyed the moment for a few more minutes before we began the trek back to the RV.

The stop was good for the soul.

I savored the few miles back to the highway on the hilly road lined with pine trees and hardwoods, with branches draping against the boundary of the road. Exiting the forest was like leaving the oasis for the desert. We were back on the four-lane highway, with the median and sides of the road periodically barren. We drove through New England as fast as we could. It was Maine or bust so we kept on trucking. Little did I know, the real adventure was about to begin.

We exited Portsmouth, New Hampshire while still on Interstate 95, and crossed the Piscataqua River entering Kittery, Maine. I knew the area like the back of my hand. I had frequented this road as a young boy while heading to Wells, Maine to spend time each summer at my uncle Dick and Aunt Linda's beach house. I also spent a lot of time there as a high school teen, mainly during the spring of my senior year. The beach was the place to go for a break from school as we sped toward graduation, and Maine was a better place for us to skip school as there were no New Hampshire truant officers there. We usually ended up on Short Sands or Long Sands beach. But on this day, we would continue about fifty-five miles north through Portland, leave I-95 as it stayed inland a bit, and hop onto Interstate 295 north. Once we reached Brunswick, Maine, we'd catch the old Route 1 which hugged the coast and led us through towns like Bath, Damariscotta, and Waldoboro, right into Rockland, which bordered Owls Head, our final destination.

About the time we hit Wiscasset, I hollered back to Joshua that I was going to look for dinosaurs in the woods as we drove along. The Jurassic Park series, written by Michael Crichton and directed by Steven Spielberg, was pretty much Joshua's favorite. He was still young enough to fantasize about whether dinosaurs were still alive. After all, it certainly could be true, and what better place for dinosaurs to hide than in the forests of Maine. Well, when Joshua heard me mention dinosaurs, his energy spiked, and he wanted to sit in the front seat of the RV and scope it out with me. I quickly obliged and pulled over to transfer Joshua from the queen-size bed in the back of the RV to the passenger's seat front and center, right beside me. I was one proud papa, driving through the Maine woods with my road dog, scoping out the forest for the dreaded Tyrannosaurus Rex. Would we find one? It took all I had not to stare at the huge smile on Joshua's face as we barreled down the road toward Owls Head. Joshua's eyes were as wide as saucers looking out the side window, and occasionally, his arms would flail and point toward the woods, and he'd say, "There's one Dad!" I was thrilled that Joshua had the strength and energy to ride in the front seat with his old man.

I look back on the moment as I write, and my throat cramps up. My eyes well up with tears…This was the only time Joshua ever sat up in the front seat of any vehicle we rode in. The memory is as clear as day nearly fifteen years later. The picture Alison snapped that day while Joshua was sitting in that front seat captures it all. He was a young boy, doing what young boys do. He was looking for dinosaurs.

It was late July when we arrived in Owls Head. Nurse Linda told us about a story she'd read about blueberry picking in Maine. Because of her story, we decided that we were going to spend a day at an orchard picking blueberries. It dawned on me that I'd not been on a family vacation in late July for years. Retirement from the NFL allowed me the luxury of joining my family on this trip.

We all loaded into the RV and ventured inland a bit from the Penobscot Bay area, west of Camden about thirty minutes. The countryside was in full bloom, and we drove through cleared fields and then narrow roads covered by a canopy of tree branches filled with the new growth of summer. I followed the sign that said "Apple Orchard" and took a right onto a country dirt road that led us through the woods to the orchard. We emerged into a clearing, and just ahead, the road was lined on both sides with apple trees. The trees were so full of apples that the branches hung down into the sides of the road. I can tell you that years ago, when they were measuring the distance to plant the trees off the side of the road, they were not thinking of the side view mirrors of our RV. As we drove down the dirt road that was little more than a trail to the barn where they processed the harvest, the branches loaded with apples clunked against our side view mirrors, and then raked along the side of the RV. Up ahead, we saw an old barn in a clearing. The apple trees gave way to a small dirt parking lot that could hold just a few vehicles at a time. Fortunately, there were no other patrons there that day, and I took the liberty of using the entire length of the lot to park the RV. The barn was at the base of a small hill that was blue due to the quantity of blueberries ready to harvest.

It was too early in the summer for apple picking, but the blueberries were full and ripe and ready for plucking. The only problem was that the bushes were up the hill a way, and I wasn't sure if Joshua's wheelchair could traverse the terrain. Everyone tumbled out of the RV, and I took Joshua's wheelchair out and set it beside the RV door. I went back in, picked Joshua up, carried him down the steps and out the door and set him up in his wheelchair. Now, remember we mentioned we wanted to give Joshua normal experiences? Well, normal for him was not usually normal for us. Sometimes the situation called for a little ingenuity, and this was one of those times. Joshua's wheelchair could not possibly roll over the rough pathway up the hill to the blueberry bushes. So I told Josh to hold on, turned his chair around and tilted him back. I then proceeded to practically drag his chair up the side of the hill backwards. Josh happily reclined in his chair and enjoyed the ride. As I pulled his chair up the hill, Linda laid her hand on Josh and made sure he did not bounce out of the chair, which would have caused quite the calamity.

After about fifty yards of bumps and bounces, we hit a perfect level spot to set Joshua up. The blueberry bushes were just the right height for Joshua to reach out and start picking, so he did. Linda sat with Joshua, Alison and Amanda started to climb to the top of the hill, and Elsie and I dispersed to find the best bushes to pick from. Within minutes, I looked up and saw Alison and Amanda about 100 yards away, about to summit the hill. I found Elsie nestled in one of the bushes filling up her container, and behind, I saw Joshua with a big smile on his face as Linda helped him pick the berries.

I took the moment to rest a bit, and to contemplate our situation. We'd driven nearly 2,000 miles to visit family and to have a family vacation. I was exhausted after the long trek but genuinely thankful that we could give Joshua an experience like this. Joshua was picking blueberries on a hillside in Maine on a beautiful summer day. For those brief hours, I was able to pretend we were normal. For a moment, we were not fighting against the time clock of life for our son.

The one clock we were fighting was Alison's biological clock. She was born with a yearning to have many children. Although the genetic possibilities loomed, she still could not shake the desire to have another baby. Maybe she would be blessed with a daughter to complete a type of *normalcy* for her soul? The prayers flowed freely and daily for the blessings of another child.

CHAPTER 11

EIGHTEEN DAYS
Paul

Joshua was in intensive care. He was fighting for his life. He had been losing weight slowly the previous two months. We knew we had to stop this trend because if he got sick with low body weight, he would have no reserve to fight against illness. Our worst nightmare was being realized. Joshua was on a ventilator, both lungs collapsed from a bout of pneumonia, lying in the intensive care unit motionless, fighting for his life. At eight years old, Joshua had already defied odds numerous times. But this time seemed different.

We were at Wolfson's Children's Hospital back in Jacksonville. Dr. Kasoon, or "Tex," as his associates fondly addressed him, was a tall, slender, handsome man from the Philippines. He lectured all over the world, and from what the staff told us, he was ranked the seventh best critical care doctor in the world.

When we arrived at the hospital with Joshua, we conducted the usual X-rays, blood tests, and many procedures needed to monitor his state. Joshua was in trouble and Dr. Kasoon knew it all too well. After a day of testing and monitoring, Tex invited us to his conference room to discuss Joshua's care. We had been under this doctor's care before, and he was very familiar with Joshua's fragile state. Tex knew that as parents we wrestled with the issue of putting Josh on permanent life support. It was a topic we'd struggled with ever since the beginning of his life. We weren't alone in our fight. Every parent faced with a fatal malady in their children grapples with this decision.

We were conflicted with the fact that permanent life support might give him extra time, but what about quality of life? How do you decide if you are prolonging life or delaying death? Do we put him on a ventilator now? He'd defied the odds of MTM and up to this point was breathing on his own. Where is that space between what modern medicine is capable of and pretending we can override the hand of God? I don't know. I still don't know.

We have friends around the world whose children have been on life support since they were born. We love them and we support their decision. But was that the best course for us? For Joshua? We didn't know.

We have other friends who chose not to prolong life mechanically. We love them, and we supported their decision. But was that the best course for us? For Joshua? We didn't know.

I will never, and could never, judge another parent for their decisions here. The right answer is so individual in nature. And honestly, I'm not sure that there is a right answer. We prayed and felt that God had Joshua's life in his hands. If God wanted Joshua on this earth, He would sustain him. If he wanted to take him home to heaven and give him a new body, it would be futile for us to try and impose our will.

Barbara K Smith, a PT from the University of Florida who has extensive experience in ICU and clinical care shares:

> Home-based mechanical ventilation has been described as the most complex medical intervention used outside of a healthcare setting. When a loved-one struggles to breathe in the ICU, families face an anguishing decision on whether or not to use life-saving mechanical ventilation using an invasive tracheostomy tube. No choice is optimal; each option carries risks for an inadequate response or other serious medical complications. The decision whether to use a life-saving therapy such as invasive ventilation should be guided by the best available medical evidence, but ultimately these care decisions are also extremely personal. While it is critical to consider how to best inflate the lungs to support life, many

other issues also contribute to the decision. These factors include but are not limited to the availability of qualified complex care providers in the home, nearby emergency medical services, the impact of invasive ventilation on the patient's ability to speak and swallow, and how to optimize communication and relationships with parents, siblings, teachers, and peers. Families cannot make these difficult decisions without considering their spiritual needs and beliefs. Once healthcare professionals counsel patients and families of the benefits and risks of each option and provide the resources needed to reach an informed conclusion, our job is then to respect and support families as they implement their decision.

The second day in the hospital, Tex sat us down in his conference room. It was a fairly sterile setting with a long office style table and some comfortable chairs to sit in. He began speaking very quietly. He told us that Joshua had no reserve. He said that he was skin and bones and his ability to fight this pneumonia was very limited. We could certainly understand his concern as we could see that very little flesh covered his rib cage. His arms and legs were perpetually skinny due to MTM. Tex told us he felt that Joshua would not make it through this illness. He thought that it was only a matter of time before Joshua's strength dissipated and his body gave way. He also said that they would do all they could and then he discussed options to bring comfort to Joshua. Tex was a profound supporter of life, but he felt that Joshua's journey would be ending soon, very soon. Alison and I were holding hands. Tears eventually gave way to chest heaving sobs as we mourned the imminent death of our son, even though he lay in his bed peacefully, just fifty feet away, letting the ventilator breathe for him. Tex stood up and gently put his hands on our shoulders. He told us to take as much time as we needed and that he would be outside if we needed him.

The next few days were filled with phone calls to family and friends. We told them of the dire circumstances and that we were probably going to have to make a decision over the next few days. All the while, Joshua lay there sleeping peacefully. We knew he was comfortable as the ventilator was forcing air into his lungs. Alison and I took turns hugging him while he lay in bed. We would lean over the rail of his bed and drape ourselves over him as we whispered in his ear how much he was loved and what a good boy he was. He had brought so much meaning to our lives. We would go through times of great faith and speak life over Joshua. We knew the power of our God, and we knew that he had given Joshua breath in his lungs since the day he was born. We also believe that our God was sovereign and that our days are numbered. But still, we begged God to bring our son through this.

Joshua's status did not change much over the first seven days of our stay. He was semi-comatose, resting peacefully but responding to us slightly when he would awaken. Tex invited us into his office again and told us that he felt things had not changed. He exuded compassion as he talked us through the issues we had to face.

We left that room weary and frayed, searching for answers and direction. We called our genetic researchers at Boston Children's Hospital. Our lead doctor was in England for a conference and we begged the switchboard in Boston to contact him. They did. When I got the doctor on the phone, I explained Joshua's status and begged him to tell me that they had made advancements in research. I was desperate for a sliver of hope. I sensed the frustration in his voice when he sternly told me that there was nothing he could do. I can only imagine what he felt when dealing with a patient's parents who were begging him to do what only God could do; bring healing to their son.

Our families began to arrive over the next couple of days to be with us. Alison, the woman of action that she is, began to talk with me about taking Joshua off the ventilator and giving him a chance to breathe on his own. I knew we were going to have to face this, and she was concerned about the issue of Joshua becoming too dependent on the machine to breathe for him. We understood the longer Joshua stayed on the ventilator, the more difficult it would be to get him off. We knew that if we didn't transition him back to his baseline—the ability to breathe on his own—there would be no option other than permanent life support.

We both decided it was time. It was day twelve. On day thirteen we were going to take Joshua off the ventilator and put him on his BiPap, a non-invasive machine with nasal prongs that would give Josh breathing assistance. We called our friends who were on this journey with us and told them what we were going to do. We told them that we were not sure what would happen and invited them to be with Joshua and us.

Tex, being aware of our decision, brought us into a small, comfortable family room to talk with us one more time. Alison, myself, her mother, and my father sat together and listened while Tex talked us through what was about to happen. Tex assured us that Joshua would be comfortable through the process. He said that when we put Joshua on the BiPap, it would take a few minutes for Joshua's CO_2 levels to raise to the point that Joshua would peacefully slip off to sleep. Tex said that Joshua's heart would then stop. Again, we began to have a barrage of mixed emotions. We prayed for God to give Joshua the strength to breathe even as we mourned the inevitable passing of our son. Tex, Elsie, and my dad filed out of the room. Alison and I remained, holding each other, and questioning if we were making the right decision. The decision not to put Joshua on permanent life support.

We left the room together and started the fifty-foot walk to Joshua's room. As we approached his suite, we saw close to thirty familiar faces that belonged to friends and family. We walked toward Joshua's room and stopped just outside. We stepped back from the entrance of his room to question our approach one more time. We quietly held each other, whispering to each other our fears; asking each other to give assurance. Were we doing the right thing? Tired, confused, and utterly drained of all strength, we stood there for what seemed like an eternity. We were just a pile of emotions. I had never experienced pain and anguish like I experienced at that moment. I held Alison close and told her I felt strongly about our decision and that we were doing the right thing for Joshua. I told her one more time that God was totally in control, and if He wanted Joshua here with us, He would give life. He would breathe for Joshua and bring him through this. It was out of our control. We were to go in that room and pray for Joshua; pray that God would give him strength to breathe, period.

As we entered the room, everyone fell silent. We were focused on Joshua and what we had to do. It was time.

Linda, Joshua's nurse who had been with us since we came to Jacksonville when Joshua was eight months old, was going to assist us as we exchanged the ventilator for the BiPap machine. She and Alison were synchronized; as Joshua was extubated, they immediately started to connect him to the BiPap. The head strap for the BiPap was awkward at best, due to the way it wrapped around Joshua's head. They fumbled with the strap for what seemed like an eternity to get the BiPap in place and functioning correctly, but after just a few seconds, the transfer was complete. Now, the waiting game began.

There were many in that room who were praying with us, standing in agreement, hoping for the miraculous to take place. Several minutes went by and Joshua's STATs remained stable. He was comfortable, not getting any better, but not showing signs of getting worse. Alison and I stood by Joshua's side. As the twenty-minute mark neared, we were cautiously optimistic. The doctors were standing in the doorway, and I went over to talk to them as Alison stayed by Joshua's side. Although Joshua was fighting and not losing ground, they assured me it was only a matter of time. They said he was simply not strong enough to come out of this.

I heard what they were saying but I wasn't listening. If Joshua could pass that few minute mark, and then the approaching twenty-minute mark, then who could say what was going to happen? We'd seen Joshua defy all odds before. I felt in my spirit that this was no exception. The doctors began to file out as they had other patients to tend. They didn't expect Joshua to recover, so they suspended all blood tests to check his CO_2 levels as they thought it was a futile exercise to do so.

Two hours later, Joshua woke up. Linda's daughter, Mary, who Joshua had grown up with, was nearby. Joshua saw her and got her attention. She hurried to his side, and within a few minutes, they were coloring together like they'd done many times before. Neither of them knew what joy they brought to us while they played together.

Two days went by. Alison and I could see changes for the better in Joshua's condition but the doctors still gave us little reason for hope. Alison asked that they take blood gases to determine the CO_2 level in Josh's blood. They reluctantly agreed.

I'll never forget Dr. Gayle's face as he returned with the results. He was smiling and shaking his head. "I don't know what's happening here, but Joshua's CO_2 levels aren't that bad." Alison and I knew what was happening; God was not finished with Joshua here on this earth. We felt strongly that Joshua would continue to improve.

We brought Joshua home five days after we took him off that ventilator and he was back in school a few days after that. This whole ordeal served to increase our faith in God. He had a plan for Joshua; one that we couldn't predict but one we had to walk through. We were reminded of this daily as each day came and went, and our Joshua thrived.

CHAPTER 12

A RISK WORTH TAKING

Alison

I come from a large family, so it was perfectly normal for me to dream of having many children. I knew that I would have a tribe of my own. I dreamed of a home full of laughter and the pitter-patter of feet running down the hallway. My home as I grew up was loud, chaotic, and filled with laughter and adventure. One day I would give that gift to my children; I just knew it. Paul was from a large family as well. We were going to have four to five children. We agreed upon that. I was headed toward my dream.

Then Joshua was born.

He changed everything. How could he not? The core of my being changed as his mom. Everything I had went toward keeping him alive. Dreams didn't matter; my life didn't matter. He was the only thing that mattered to me. And it stayed that way for a long time, for a couple of years. But eventually, I had to face my new reality. I had to reckon with dreams of the past. I had to grieve this dream; I would not be a mother to multiple children. But maybe..., I could have one more?

I knew in my heart a girl was waiting. I had seen her; I knew of her before I was even married. I could feel her presence. I can't explain it, but every mother would understand this. Maybe, she was still waiting for me? But oh my God, the risk! What if I had another baby like Joshua, afflicted with MTM? Could I keep two alive; what if the baby didn't make it? I knew that no matter what any tests showed, I would choose life, but what was I signing up for? What was I risking for that baby? Would it be fair to a child, knowing I carried the gene?

All these fears swirled in my mind. It took me years to make sense of them. But eventually, five years after Joshua was born, it settled in my heart. I decided it was worth the risk. My girl was worth the risk.

I mustered the courage to schedule an appointment with a fertility doctor. I was hoping he would give us ways to control the outcome of a healthy pregnancy. If I was going to do this, I had to use every tool available. I sat in his office, and he explained the different ways that fertility doctors can increase your chances of having a healthy child. I realized while sitting there that deep in my gut, I could not choose life or death. Even as I leaned toward one of the options he gave me, at the end of the day, this decision would be in the hands of God. Producing a healthy baby is not something I could control. However, let me say here, that it is an option that many women courageously choose to grow their family. I love that these options exist, but in that moment, they were not right for me.

It wouldn't have mattered, he refused to take my case. I was too high risk.

Shaken by the experience, I left his office and drove home. It had taken me years to even sit in that office. I was left with the reality that I would have a healthy child or not, but I knew I couldn't control it. Whatever happened next was in the hands of God.

Five weeks later, I made an appointment with my OBGYN, because I knew I was pregnant. It was of no surprise when they called me back, "Mrs. Frase, congratulations, you're pregnant."

Well, I knew that I could not force this life into existence, but I was going to do everything possible to keep the child healthy. I danced between peace and fear as my heart struggled to believe the promise of God for my life. Would this baby be healthy? That question was never far from my mind. But I knew, and I kept telling Paul, "I will know when I see that baby."

Our sonogram was scheduled at sixteen weeks. My emotions skyrocketed, swirling around in my body; I could not seem to land one for any length of time. Overwhelming peace followed by gut-wrenching anxiety, combined with a mother's desire to see her baby for the first time.

Thank God for modern day medicine! The team of doctors surrounded us in the room as the technician prepared my body. The room was so packed they could hardly move around. Suddenly, there she was. Legs crossed underneath her, staring right at me. And then she did something that took our breath away. She waved; her little right hand raised, and her fingers rolled from her index to her pinky in the most beautiful wave I have seen in my life. Relief flooded my soul, and Paul and I held each other and sobbed. Our baby was healthy, it was right there on the screen. The truth of that statement was staring at us, waving from behind the screen. The doctors left the room to give us privacy. The anatomy scan was perfect even though they couldn't determine the sex of the child because its legs were crossed. Because this baby's legs were crossed, and it was sitting up, this was widely different from any ultrasound I had had with Joshua. After giving us some time, the technician reentered the room to complete the ultrasound from a different angle. She confirmed what I already knew. We were having a girl.

The pregnancy was a delight. Easy and uncomplicated in every way. I won the name debate, and Paul graciously conceded. I would have my Isabella. I loved her already, I dreamed of ballet shoes side by side with Joshua's Matchbox cars. A world of pink next to his world of blue. She would have a big brother just like I did, and he would have a little sister. I couldn't wait for the joy Isabella would add to our lives. I was even looking forward to the drama. Joshua was ecstatic; he couldn't wait to be a big brother.

Her due date came and went. Twelve days later, my birthing coach told me to walk in the ocean so my body could feel the rhythm of the ebb and flow that it would need to throw me into contractions. She also told me to go eat spicy food. My mother and I walked in the Atlantic Ocean for two hours and found the spiciest Mexican food we could find. The advice did the trick. We headed down to Wolfson Children's hospital, but I was not far enough along so they sent me home.

The next morning, the doctor called and said to meet her at the hospital. It was time to induce labor. At 11:30 p.m., Isabella Patrice Frase entered the world, pink, strong, and healthy. She set my heart once and for all at peace. She was the completing piece of our family. I will never forget

Joshua entering the room in the cute little outfit I had pressed the day before. Pride and excitement shone in his eyes. I was overcome with such joy and contentment. My dream for a large family had died, but my little family was perfect in every way.

While the dream was dead, a void still existed in my heart. I would go on to love the MTM warriors in place of the children I never had. They filled the void.

CHAPTER 13

A DAY IS A DAY
Paul

When Joshua was about nine years old, we were watching a show on the Discovery Channel about natural disasters. The show covered real life occurrences like Hurricane Andrew that hit Homestead, Florida in the early 90s and a category F5 tornado that hit some midwestern state and left total devastation in its wake. It talked about the two-day eruption of Mount Vesuvius that destroyed Pompeii in 79 AD, and about how the 1980 eruption of Mt. St. Helens in Washington State had an effect on weather all over the world.

After the show was over, Joshua began to wonder out loud which natural catastrophe could cause the most devastation. He thought that earthquakes were intense, but that Tsunamis could cause widespread destruction. He also asked me about those, "things that come out of the sky and hit the earth. You know, Dad, those big rock things."

"Do you mean meteorites, Josh?"

"Yeah, Dad, meteorites! They can be really dangerous!" Joshua asked me what I thought was the worst natural catastrophe and I told him that, to me, a Category 5 hurricane would be the hardest to deal with. I received a nod of approval for my answer and then Joshua looked at me and said, "Well, Dad, a day is a day, and some days are dangerous."

I laughed out loud and repeated his statement, "Yes, Josh, you're right. A day is a day, and some days are dangerous."

Our *days* and our *dangerous days* with this rare disease are so interwoven that most *dangerous days* started out looking no different than ordinary days. We have meteorologists to forecast the approaching hurricane. There is never a warning for parents like us. Alison and I lived with a perpetual state of catastrophe lurking right around the corner. What I didn't tell Joshua that day was, even living in Florida, it wasn't a Category 5 hurricane that I feared the most. In fact, compared to what I considered a dangerous day, I would almost welcome a hurricane.

A year before that conversation with my son, Alison and I were headed up to St. Simon's Island, Georgia for the day, hoping to leave reality behind us and soak in the restorative powers of a relaxing day away. It was 8:38 a.m.; we were fifteen minutes away from home and forty-five minutes away from our first stop at the Ritz Carlton in Amelia Island. We were planning on a nice brunch served outside on the deck when the phone rang.

I could tell by the tone in the nurse's voice that something was drastically wrong. Josh had stopped breathing. The nurse was normally cool and calm in every circumstance, but this was different. "He's not breathing! He's turning blue!"

Alison asked, "Have you called 911?"

"Yes, they are on their way! I've got to go... I've got to go..."

Alison screamed at the top of her lungs, "Wait! What happened?"

The nurse replied that Josh had a mucous plug while he was in the bathtub, and when she ran to get the suction machine, his face had turned to the side. "I've got to go use the Ambu bag!"

Alison yelled, "Go, go, go.... We're on our way!" And then she screamed to get the car turned around and get home. I was already making an illegal U-turn through the median of a four-lane highway.

I'm very conservative by nature, sometimes too conservative. It spills over to my driving style, whereas Alison likes everything done in a New York minute. I prefer to take my time and mosey on down the road. This was the exception. With my wife begging God to spare our son's life, and my mind racing about what was happening at our home, I cut across the median and forced my way into oncoming rush hour traffic. I pounded the accelerator and sucked every ounce of power I could out of that engine. As I forced my way onto A1A, I began to weave in and out of traffic. Traffic was about four cars deep at the red light. I swerved to the right, found an opening, and cut all the way to the left across three lanes onto the breakdown strip of pavement. Fortunately, there were no cars as I raced to the left of the standing traffic onto the grass, running the red light and screaming past everyone with my hazard lights flashing and my horn blasting.

To be miles away from your son as he fights for his life is a loss of control that simply cannot be described, and it's a feeling that I've felt one too many times. "Call home!" I yelled at Alison. She had already dialed the house and was screaming at the phone for the nurse to pick up. The nurse answered the phone and told Alison that she had revived Josh and that he was breathing with the assistance of the Ambu bag. This was not good at all. "Are the paramedics there yet? No? Is he okay?"

The nurse replied, "He's stable but I'm afraid he might have aspirated. I've got to go! I've got to work on him."

Alison was in overdrive as she told the nurse we were almost there and to "Keep him alive!"

As we raced home running red lights and alarming the other drivers on the road, my mind went into the kind of zone that most people only read about. Everything around my peripheral vision became blurry and I had clarity only in the center of my sight. The focus seemed intense, and I was hearing Alison yell and pray at the top of her lungs, but it seemed like I was a hundred miles away. As we pulled into our community, my mind snapped back into real time. We saw the flashing lights of the ambulance parked in front of our house. Alison was jumping out of the car and bounding into the house before I even came to a complete stop. I slammed the car into park and raced into the house right behind her, dodging the EMTs in the garage and pushing a couple of guys aside to get into our son's bedroom. Alison had already jumped up on the bed and started assisting with Joshua's care. Joshua was still an ashen gray color and glassy eyed. He was not responding and had that vacant look in his eyes.

Alison started to whisper in his ear, "Mommy is here, Josh; Mommy is here. Stay with us, Josh. It's okay, Mommy is here; stay with us."

Joshua was listless, not responding at all to our presence. We had the oxygen flowing at fifteen liters per minute and still we weren't getting a response. We had to be careful; his CO_2 levels were obviously very high. At this point, he was barely with us. In this condition, you had to control how much oxygen you were giving him, because too much would have the same effect as not enough. His CO_2 levels would slowly rise, and he would *fall asleep*. Essentially, he would pass out and then your main concern is Joshua falling into a coma. After that, with every second that passes the possibility of something going very wrong increases drastically.

The EMTs were not familiar with us yet as we'd only been living in the area for a few months. The EMTs in Atlantic Beach, our previous neighborhood for five years, knew us by name. It was always tough to get them to understand that we needed to instruct them on how to handle Joshua. We knew an EMT was good by their ability to recognize that we knew what we were doing and when they would ask us questions about Joshua's care. At times, we'd run into a medical professional that had total disregard for what we had to say concerning our son's care. They were strictly *by the book* and very obstinate in their ways. This would only add fuel to a very intense and volatile situation. We knew how critical it was to administer help to Joshua correctly. Many times, Joshua was so fragile that we only had seconds to respond or his life was at risk. We were not going to lose our son because of the ignorance of others involved, no matter their experience, and often we found ourselves taking over and teaching by example. The EMTs that joined us that morning understood quickly that the mother and father of this child were heavily involved with his care, and they could rely on the information we were giving them. God bless those EMTs.

It took about fifteen minutes to get Joshua stable enough to transport him out to the ambulance on a gurney. During that time, the EMTs called for a life flight helicopter and radioed to have them meet us at a church right down the road. Alison rode in the ambulance to meet the helicopter and managed to persuade the flight commander that she needed to join them on the flight. It was vital for her to comfort Joshua and instruct the EMTs how to care for him. I heard her say, "You need me on your team, I know him better than anyone."

Once they arrived at the ER, for a brief moment, Joshua came to and asked Alison what happened to him. He told her that he started to cough, but then couldn't remember anything after that. This was the first time that Joshua could not recall the incident that led to a hospitalization, and his lack of recall confirmed for Alison the nurse's suspicion that Joshua drowned. Trying not to scare him, Alison told Josh that he'd drowned and that they were working on helping him get better. Josh accepted the information and slipped back into his lethargic state.

We had a long day with Josh as he fought for his life tooth and nail. He was listless well into the night and slept without responding to us. We were really concerned because his X-rays showed that both lungs had collapsed and we were ready for the doctors to fight to put him on a ventilator, an intervention we always pushed hard against. He was on his BiPap, and for the time being, it was doing the job. Josh eventually showed signs of recovery. Alison had been running on adrenaline for hours and was showing signs of severe fatigue. I convinced her that Josh was going to come out of this one too, and she needed to go home and get some sleep so that one of us would be somewhat refreshed in the morning to take whatever the next day might hand us. She left the hospital around 10 p.m., and I started my nightly routine for a hospital stay with my son.

When Joshua was in this state, he was usually too weak to give out more than a very quiet cry. I was always afraid that this cry was not loud enough to wake me, so I usually only fell asleep for an hour at a time, here and there. I also left one of his Matchbox cars beside his hand so that if he woke and needed me, he could pick up the car and bang it on the metal bars on the side of the bed. At 2:12 in the morning, almost eighteen hours after receiving the frantic phone call, I awoke suddenly to the pinging sound of metal on metal. I jumped off the chair and stood up to see Josh wide awake, his eyes wide open, and a smile on his face. I was still groggy and wanted to sleep, but I could tell Josh wanted to talk. Because of the dire circumstances of the day, I wasn't going to miss out on this opportunity to have a conversation with my son.

Joshua started with, "How are you doing, Dad?" and I could only respond that I was doing all right, considering what had just happened. I will never forget his next words, "Dad, I'm glad I'm still here."

I was blown away. What do I say to my eight-year-old son who had just fought for his life for eighteen hours and won today's battle against death? All I could think to say was, "Well, Josh, I'm glad you're still here too."

"Yeah," he said, "but I'm glad I didn't die today." After catching my breath and again, feeling that just any answer might be inadequate, I decided to use this open door as a teaching tool and spread my *infinite* knowledge about life and death with my son. So, at 2:30 a.m., in an intensive care unit, relieved and grateful, I started to tell Josh that someday, we were all going to die, and that those of us who put our faith and trust in God and his son Jesus would one day see each other and our loved ones in heaven.

In an innocent manner, Josh stated, "Yeah, but not until I'm old like Nanna." Josh's Nanna was around seventy-two at the time.

Not bad expectations for a boy whom doctors said wouldn't survive his first day. To this day, that statement remains one of the most profound and thought-provoking moments between us. It's made me reflect on the finite and somewhat closed-minded response that put my son's life in a box by putting a limit on his life and what he might accomplish. All of us will die one day. None of us know when. Some of us are confined by our thoughts, words, and deeds, and some of us are defined by our thoughts, words and deeds. That night, my words were confining, and Joshua's words were defining. His words carried him a lot further than mine.

CHAPTER 14

THE SCIENCE

Alison

We all have a job to do here on earth. Some of us find it earlier than others. Some don't find it until late in life. But I believe that we're all here for a greater purpose than what we know. Would I have carried on if Joshua passed before our first breakthrough? I don't know. Here's what I do know.

Joshua had a story to tell. Joshua had a purpose. There was an undercurrent between us—I needed Joshua to stay alive because he gave me the courage to press on, and he needed us to find a way to make that happen.

There was a tension between God and me, and I know that I'm not supposed to talk about him so much in this book. But, for this, I must. I had to believe that there was a reason for Joshua's existence. I would yell at the heavens, "Tell me his life isn't in vain! Tell me that there's a reason he's like this. Show me. Show me your purposes in all of this."

It's hard to feel like your son is a sacrificial lamb. It's even harder when you spend every day of your life trying to find ways to raise money, so that you can hand that money to researchers who will maybe, hopefully, at some point, possibly ask the right questions that will maybe, hopefully, at some point, possibly lead to the right answers. We had to trust the process and hope that we would eventually taste the fruit of our labor.

It took years for us to find our first scientific breakthrough. It was almost a decade. To help spur on research, I called tissue banks around the country asking for muscle samples which Alan Beggs, our lead geneticist at Boston Children's, could work with. I also called families encouraging participation in Alan's efforts, assuring them that the more information we learned about this disorder, the better off we'd be. For nine years we sent check after check to Alan and his team at Boston Children's Hospital, and they went to work in their labs. Tucked between microscopes, they asked questions like, "So there is a genetic defect that caused the muscle weakness, so, let's locate the defective gene and fix the problem." And other questions like, "Would the fix be with an existing small molecule pharmaceutical, or could we design a new genetic therapy that would work?" They eventually asked the question, "Could we locate the defective gene and use gene replacement therapy, hopefully eliminating the issues of myotubular myopathy?" And when they asked that question, they struck gold.

Because Alan believed so strongly that science moves faster when scientists collaborate, he naturally reached out to others. His reach spread across the Atlantic where he met Dr. Anna Buj-Bello, a researcher in France working on mice with a mutation in the MTM1 gene that encodes the myotubularin protein. This mutation "knocks out" the function of myotubularin, allowing scientists to ask the all-important question: Is myotubularin necessary for muscle function and how does the muscle become defective if this protein is absent?

Alan and I were talking with each other one day when I asked him, "What are we doing? What's the next thing?" When he told me about Anna and her mice, I offered to pay to bring them to America. Alan and Anna began to work out how to get the mice here, and eventually, in 2005, we established our first mouse colony at Boston Children's Hospital.

Two years later he sent me an email with a video link in it. The video showed a mouse affected with the same disorder Joshua has, dragging his legs behind him. After one shot of gene therapy, the Knockout Mouse was running around his cage with no sign of debilitating muscle issues. Tears spontaneously flowed down my cheeks, which is ridiculous, because I was watching a video about a mouse! When was the last time a mouse made you cry? It was certainly a first for me!

Anna published her work in 2007, and when that happened, we had our first proof of concept with the science. All of the years our researchers spent tucked away in laboratories, asking questions—discovering traits of

X-linked myopathies, and working to understand the complexities of this disorder—they all led to this, our first pinnacle of research. But it wasn't enough to approach the FDA. Our conversations changed from, "Where do we go from here?" to "We will never get from a mouse to a human. We need a dog." Without a dog, we were at a stalemate.

It was the third Thursday in March of 2008, and we were winding down our tenth JFF Muscle Dream Team Gala. It would be the first gala to feel the weight of the recession that had begun months before on Wall Street. I didn't know it yet, but it would be the lowest margin of profit we'd experienced since we'd first begun raising money for research. After the following year, I would abandon the gala altogether, but those cards weren't on the table yet. That night, all I knew is that we were having a great time and Peter Wolf was doing a phenomenal job entertaining the crowd.

Alan caught up to me in the hallway before we entered the gala for the closing ceremonies of the night. We had to raise our voices to hear one another. When Alan said, "I think we have possibly found a dog," time stood still. Everything went into a fog.

Did I just hear him correctly? I yelled over the loud music, "Did you just say we might have a dog?"

His reply hit me like a ton of bricks, "Yes, Alison, one of my colleagues that I met at a conference shared with me that she thinks she's looking at a canine muscle sample that resembles MTM under the microscope. I offered her my help, but she declined my offer." My world stopped. Could this be the huge break we'd been waiting for? Could this dog really be a carrier, a mama dog who carried the same gene that I did? Alan congratulated me on another amazing job on another successful event. As we were walking out, I asked Alan to follow up in the morning and introduce me to this researcher.

The rest of that night was a blur for me. I didn't know whether to laugh or to cry. I'll never forget feeling the weight of hope that night. My skin tingled with possibilities. The hope for a cure was so tangible. Maybe Josh wouldn't have to die. Maybe, just maybe, we were going to beat that damn clock that had been ticking since the day he was born. I needed this dog like I needed the next breath I would take, and like the next breath my son would take. Our lives hung in the balance. I woke that next morning with the knowing that I have received many times prior. I knew I needed to pursue this potential lead with everything I had. I felt it was a direct directive, orchestration, from above.

CHAPTER 15

SASKATOON OR BUST

Alison

Alan emailed me the next morning while I was wrapping my head around the news from the night before. The gala had been a success, but the waning stock market had taken its toll on our overall funds. Normally, I would have been reviewing and breaking down all the variables of the night, but Alan's email had me reeling just a bit. In prior years, the adrenaline ran out about 3 a.m. the morning after, but this day, I was still on the adrenaline rush well into the morning.

Alan's email was a letter of introduction to G. Diane Shelton DVM, PhD, DACVIM (Internal Medicine) and Professor in the Department of Pathology at the University of California, San Diego. Dr. Shelton was the colleague Alan had met recently at a conference, and she shared with Alan the news that she might be looking at a slide of muscle tissue that presented like Myotubular Myopathy. I was quite shocked at Dr. Shelton's response, which basically said that she would not speak with me, and it seemed that she literally wanted us to lose her email. Alan later explained that she was constantly under heavy scrutiny from animal activist organizations, which made her reaction more logical to me, especially being an animal lover myself. I had to strategize on how to win Dr. Shelton over, or at the very least, find a way to share information that would not attach to her in any way.

So, I found the phone number to her laboratory on the Internet, picked up the phone, and dialed the number. It was a slim chance, but one I was willing to take. "Hello, Diane Shelton here." I had struck gold. Not only had I gotten through to a live person, but it was also the exact person I needed to talk to! After forty-five minutes of pleading for her to look at it from my eyes, I asked her if she would please introduce me to the breeder who sent her the muscle tissue. She said she would think about it. Two weeks later, she reluctantly gave me the name of the breeder of the Toy Manchester Terrier that was possibly a MTM carrier. For the next two months, the breeder shunned every attempt I made to connect and explain our plight and our fight against the clock. She would have nothing to do with me. My last and final attempt to contact this breeder was a flight to California to plead my case face to face. Mercifully, right before I booked the flight, Dr. Shelton received another possible tissue sample of an affected puppy from a vet named Dr. Snead who practiced in Saskatoon, Saskatchewan—the Canadian province that straddles Montana and North Dakota. The sample was from a Labrador retriever named Trixie. I asked Dr. Shelton to approach the owners about possibly breeding Trixie for me and or testing her to see *if* she was an MTM carrier.

Everything was falling into place. The vivarium that WFIRM had been working on was finally completed just a month before. Dr. Atala had recently added a doctor to his team who'd been a lead in canine preclinical trials for the past twenty years. Prior to accepting the job at WFIRM, Dr. Martin K. Childers, who goes by Casey, worked with Joe Kornegay at the University of Missouri leading canine research for Duchenne muscular dystrophy. I did not need to reinvent the wheel, so I handed the job off to Alan and Casey to contact the owners of Trixie. Paul would later say this was very uncharacteristic of me with my take-charge and unrelinquishing ways. But I was tired, and I needed a bit of rest after pulling off a huge event and working the last four months to find the dog that could lead us to a cure.

Alan initiated the introductory emails and then left for vacation. Upon his return two weeks later, he emailed Casey about his ventures and success in retrieving *the dog*. When Casey replied, "What dog," Alan kicked it into high gear. He quickly surmised that the spam filters for the WFIRM's servers were blocking any correspondence regarding the dog because the veterinarians were using the word "bitch" while discussing Trixie and the retrieval. The word "bitch" was commonly used as it refers to a female dog, and the spam filters picked it up as derogatory language and blocked the emails.

Alan promptly reengaged via emails and phone calls, and Dr. Snead called the owner of Trixie to apologize that we'd not been in touch. The owner shared his concern with her and related that he just couldn't bear to have Trixie run away and get pregnant like she had previously, so he'd had her spayed. When she relayed the information to me, I couldn't believe what I was hearing; our only hope vanished into thin air. We went from having a potential dog, to no dog. It was hard enough finding peers of Joshua's, never mind another dog with MTM. This was like finding a microscopic needle in a haystack.

I was in shock when I hung up the phone and told Paul about the devastating news. Paul reminded me that it was uncharacteristic of me to relinquish control, but that there must be a reason. He took me by the shoulders and made sure he had my full attention, saying "The next dog we find, you are getting on an airplane, and you are going to get that dog." I was in full agreement with him, but how would we find another? When would we find another?

And then I had an idea.

I immediately called Elizabeth Snead, the vet in Canada, knowing that she might have information about Trixie's family line. Being that my family bred German shepherds as a child, it was a chance that maybe we could track her lineage. As fate would have it, Canada is known for keeping extensive records of canine family trees, and Trixie led Dr. Snead to a few possibilities. She called me back a few weeks later and told me that she'd found relatives of Trixie and had left messages on the answering machines of five people who may have owned one of Trixie's relatives. One person called her back, a man by the name of Vic Wagman. He told her about his dog, and Elizabeth took his information and contacted me. She had no idea about his interest in helping if any, but she shared his phone number and gave me the green light to call Vic back. It was just days before Christmas of 2008. Before hanging up, I said to Elizabeth, this could be the best Christmas gift ever.

It was quite an unusual call for Vic to receive, and when I look back on it, I must have sounded quite desperate. But, just five minutes into my impassioned plea, Vic stopped me and said, "I want to give you my dog, I want to help your son." Once again, time seemed to stand still. I must have said thank you 100 times over the next few minutes. Vic had to stop me again and said, "You need to come right away and get her. She runs with about twenty-five horses and accidents happen here on the farm. Her name is Nibs, and she's a strong chocolate lab. The closest airport is Saskatoon which is about 3 ½ hours from my house. Set the flight, and I will meet you there with Nibs." I hung up the phone with tears in my eyes.

Five days later, on December 27, 2008, I was on a plane headed to Saskatoon. Weather was horrible that time of year, and subsequently, so was traveling. I was rerouted on several airlines, due to cancelation of flights as a massive snowstorm was to arrive exactly where I was headed. I arrived to meet Vic, his wife Karen, and Nibs. My luggage, and dog crate carrier however, failed to make the changes with me. I arrived to hear the news that the airport was planning to cancel all flights the next day, mid-morning, due to a massive blizzard heading their way. Nibs stayed with me that night. She instantly connected with me which Vic thought was very uncharacteristic of her. I continued to call the Northwest ticket counter asking if they located my bag and dog crate. "No, Mrs. Frase, we have not located your bags, and we advise you figure this out by morning as this place will be shut down soon. Also be advised that if the temperature drops below 28 degrees below zero, you will not be able to fly with the animal."

I woke knowing what I needed to do. I threw on the clothes I traveled in and called Vic. Vic and his wife Karen took me to purchase traveling necessities for Nibs. Running through the pet store, I looked at the size of the crate, thinking this will be a good size for Nibs. So, in the customs lobby, we assembled the dog crate with a three-inch screwdriver with the guy at the ticket counter pointing at his watch, "Hurry, Alison, or you're going to miss this flight." Providence was working overtime on my behalf that morning; the temperature that morning only fell to 23 degrees below zero, and I had no idea the crate size needed to be a specific size or smaller to fit the cargo door on the plane, but we made both. I hugged them goodbye with tears in my eyes as my girl and I boarded the last plane out of Saskatoon. This blizzard closed the airport for the next week, but we were on our way to meet our researcher in North Carolina.

CHAPTER 16

NIBS' LEGACY; THE DOG COLONY

Alison

It is impossible for me to accurately describe the next part of our journey. Nibs and I arrived in Winston-Salem, North Carolina, and after making sure she was settled in, I had to leave her. My home was in Florida; hers would now be in North Carolina where she would become the matriarch of our dog colony. I couldn't bear the thought of her living at the research lab, so Casey and his wife took her in until I could make arrangements with a local breeder for her to live on a farm. Nibs, in my opinion, belonged on a farm. Aside from constant communication with our researchers, pictures sent via email, and the sporadic trips I was able to make up the East Coast, I was physically distant from our colony. Mandy Lockard, however, was their daily companion. We all love these dogs, but Mandy carries a special place for them in her heart. For us to let you into our world, behind doors that remain tightly closed to the public at large, this chapter needs to be told from our colony's best friend.

As told by Mandy:

My name is Mandy, and ten years ago, Myotubular Myopathy wasn't on my radar. In fact, I'd never even heard of it. I was living in Michigan with my husband, happily employed in work that I loved as a lab tech in animal laboratories. I know that there are countless horror stories of animal labs, but I also know the benefit to research they contribute, and I love it for that reason. There are good, ethical animal laboratories out there, and I've been privileged to work in them. After years of talking about it, we finally moved to North Carolina in 2005, and I found a job working at Wake

Forest in the Animal Resource Department. It is my distinct honor to contribute a chapter about the MTM dog colony, just as it was an honor to be a part of it, and an honor to know Joshua.

My entry into this story is one of pure coincidence, or perhaps it was orchestrated by a higher being. Either way, in March 2008, I was working on a blood vessel project at WFIRM and attended their annual retreat where all of the investigators get together to present their work. Dr. Martin Childers presented information on the Golden Retriever Muscular Dystrophy dogs he was working with, and I couldn't believe my ears. Did I really hear him say he was driving two hours to pick placentas up off the floor so they could collect tissue to grow in the lab?

I thought about that statement for a few days and finally went to Dr. Childers' office to let him know I could help get him fresh placentas. Not only that, but these placentas were sterile and here in town. I was working part time with Dr. Jane Barber, a local veterinary reproductive specialist, and I told him how dog breeding can be timed and C-sections scheduled as far as nearly two months in advance. He and Dr. Barber were introduced, and Dr. Childers had a new source for placentas for his project.

Placentas were exchanged; I went back to my blood vessel project, and life went on. About a year later, I heard that Dr. Childers had a dog flown in from Canada, and he needed to breed her to a Labrador Retriever. I invited myself back to his office to let him know that there was a possibility I could help him get the semen he needed, and that's when I learned about Joshua Frase for the very first time. After one failed attempt with a different breeder, I was able to connect Dr. Childers with Mrs. Lab, a breeder I knew from my work with Dr. Barber. She heard the story I was just beginning to know about a boy with a rare neuromuscular disorder, and readily agreed to let us use her stud dog. I didn't know it yet, but my life was changing right before my eyes.

Nibs was bred in February 2009 to one of Mrs. Lab's studs. In April, at a local farm and under the watchful eye of Mrs. Lab, Nibs gave us twelve puppies, four males and eight females, our Color litter. There was one affected male, "Gray Boy," and five carrier females. These carriers: Red, Black, Orange, Pink and Blue— my girls—became the foundation to the XLMTM colony. Gray Boy deteriorated quickly after fourteen weeks and crossed the Rainbow Bridge at eighteen weeks, but unaffected male and female dogs were adopted by families in the MTM community. Nibs returned to her farm in Saskatchewan, where she lived for the remainder of her days.

The girls were ready to be bred in June 2010. Once again, Mrs. Lab donated the use of her stud dog. In July, I received a call from Dr. Childers requesting a meeting. This breeding was different. The dogs were now in a research setting. This environment is tightly regulated to ensure the safety of the animals and the research. Mrs. Lab was not going to be able to whelp (deliver) this litter of pups. Dr. Childers asked if I would join his team as the Breeding Colony Manager, and I jumped at the opportunity.

Working in an animal research environment has its fair share of challenges. Strict protocols must be followed. The three Rs of research need to be respected—reduce, replace, and refine methods in order to use fewer animals. One of the ways we tried to do this was to reduce the number of dogs at the facility by shipping semen in, rather than having a male dog live at the facility. The challenge is that the lab needs to time the hormone levels of the female, collect specimen from the male, and then hope the semen will be able to be delivered when you need it. After a few shipments of dead semen, we quickly realized that this was not going to work. I sought out the assistance of Kristin Block, who specializes in freezing dog semen. The idea was to keep frozen semen stored at the university, so we would have access to quality semen when we needed to breed the girls. This partnership worked out well. Originally, we were going to have to surgically implant the semen under general anesthesia, but Kristin offered up her other expertise—transcervical insemination (TCI) —which allows us to breed the dog with no sedation.

With each litter, we anxiously await to see if the transfer is successful, and then we wait to find out if there will be any male puppies. We love every single dog individually, but Myotubular Myopathy is an X-linked disorder, and that means we need male puppies to study it. Our lab is giddy with excitement when a male is produced, but there is a sadness that comes along too. This disorder progresses quickly in dogs. We see them begin to show small signs within the first few weeks, then noticeable signs by four weeks. Simply put, they can't keep up. Puppies are boisterous and energetic, but an affected male can hardly walk across a room.

In March 2011 we had two litters—the Designer litter out of Black and the Royal litter out of Pink—aka Princess Pink. All of our litters were themed so we could easily know who was a litter mate with whom. Black gave us a nice litter of seven with two affected boys, Tommy and Giorgio. Pink had a small litter of three, but amazingly, the one male pup that she gave us was affected. His name was Buckingham. These three guys received a local injection of gene therapy into a leg muscle. We had good results with the injection, but unfortunately it did not improve their overall quality of life. Tommy and Giorgio crossed the bridge in July 2011 at the age of eighteen weeks. Buckingham also crossed in July at sixteen weeks old. Losing an animal is never easy, and we grieved their loss as a team. However, this was the first litter we were able to inject with gene therapy, and it was important to celebrate the advance of science.

During the middle of the WFIRM Halloween party on October 28, 2011, Black (from our Color litter) went into labor and gave us seven pups, only one of which was affected. We named him Rocky; what a fitting name for such a wonderful dog. Rocky was scheduled for a single leg infusion on December 20, 2011. This procedure was different from the other pups, as it would be going into the bloodstream of his rear leg, rather than into a single muscle. The procedure went smoothly and Rocky recovered uneventfully.

As with our other affected pups, we knew the road ahead and began making preparations. To everyone's amazement, Rocky was doing great. His strength measurements came back nearly identical to a normal dog. He was noticeably disabled, but his health did not deteriorate at the same rate of the past dogs. It was obvious that this boy was going to beat the odds and not only survive, but flourish. Our science was improving!

At the end of March, Black came back into season and was bred for a third time. May 23, 2012, she gave us a huge litter of ten pups, our scientist litter. Turing and Pavlov were our affected males, and both received the same therapy as Rocky. It was around this time that I knew my time with this colony was drawing to an end. Dr. Childers had accepted a position with the University of Washington, and the entire colony was going to be moved west. But we still had work to do with Rocky, Pavlov, and Turing, so we kept at it.

As Rocky progressed, a crazy idea came about. What if we can get him to live to puberty? If we bred an affected male to a carrier female, we could get affected females. As far as we knew, none had ever existed, because all the affected males die before they are sexually mature. The other outcome of this type of breeding would be the rest of the females being carriers. Producing affected females would double the number of affected dogs in a litter and therefore doubling the speed of research being done. Can you even imagine the excitement? Oh, the possibilities!

In July 2012, it was finally time to see if Rocky was becoming a man. At seven months old, we decided to attempt semen collection. Rocky performed for us, but the real test would be looking at what he gave us under a microscope. When we put the slide on the scope, we rejoiced. Not only did we have live semen, but it appeared to be normal. We prepared to start collecting and freezing semen on Rocky in hopes that we could use it to breed to a carrier. Our first attempt was a failure; the semen was all dead after freezing. As was the second, third, and fourth. We tried a variety of procedures, but never could get the semen to come back to life after being frozen.

We knew that we were working against the clock as Rocky was approaching his first birthday and the end point of his study. Realizing the value of his semen and the possibilities it held, we requested more time to try and figure out how to immortalize this dog with frozen semen. Our request was approved, and we began our search. No matter who we called, we kept getting the same response: "If it's dead, it's dead." In a last-ditch effort, I contacted the human reproductive experts at WFU. Dr. Tamer Yalcinkaya and Dr. Yimin Shu returned the email, both with quite a bit of interest. After much collaboration, Dr. Shu did a test freeze and thaw of Rocky's semen, followed by testing our new compounds. To all our astonishment, the semen wasn't actually dead, it was simply not moving. We just needed to give it a boost!

Over the month of August, my girls slowly started shipping out to Washington. Red never had regular cycles and had some allergy issues, so we decided it was best for her to be spayed and adopted. Dr. Rob Grange, one of the collaborators on the project, opened his heart and his home to her. She went to live with him on August 9, 2012.

That same day, Myrtle, Fleur, Shelly, Marie, Rosalind, and Gerty were moved to the University of Washington. August 18, 2012, my big girls left me; Black, Orange, Pink, Blue. As they left, I knew this was most likely the last time I would see them. My heart was torn, I knew they had a job to do, but I would miss them so much. Turing and Pavlov remained at WFIRM to finish up testing before being shipped to the University of Washington on October 24, 2012. Voodoo and Elvira (from the Halloween litter) stayed in NC at WFIRM to continue the breeding colony. In November 2012, there was discussion of failed breedings in WA along with the likelihood that the two girls at WFIRM would be coming into season soon. As fate would have it, I walked into the housing room a few days later and Elvira was in season. There were no plans to breed her at that point since Dr. Childers was no longer at WFIRM, but the team needed to produce pups to continue the study. After many frantic phone calls, I got the green light to breed her.

I can distinctly remember having a challenging day with my kids. When my husband walked in the door, I told him he needed to take over while I took our family dogs for a walk. It was cold, dark, and foggy. I remember being able to see the mist hanging in the air with the head lamp I was wearing. During the walk, I called Dr. Childers to discuss the upcoming breeding. I wanted to use Rocky. This was our chance to make history, and likely our only chance at using Rocky since we were having so many issues with the freezing process. Casey's response: "I was thinking the same thing."

Our discussions then turned to what we really needed out of the litter. Yes, it would be nice to make history and immortalize Rocky, but we need affected dogs. Using Rocky was a huge risk. While working with his semen, we learned it didn't live very long. It needed to live long enough to fertilize the eggs. Could it do it? We finally decided to do a dual sire breeding, using good semen from a normal dog along with Rocky's fresh collected semen. The breeding was done the day before Thanksgiving and the sixty-three-day wait was on to see if we would have puppies.

January came and so did a new year with new beginnings. Elvira was confirmed pregnant and due January 20. On January 19, I was at home monitoring her via video, and I noticed her acting differently. By 7 p.m., I was at the facility, a forty-five-mile drive away, to check on her. This girl about drove me crazy. She would dig and pant and act like a bitch in whelp, then lie down and sleep for a while, then get up and do it again. We checked her temp, which was normal, but she just wasn't acting right. We continued to monitor her with the camera from upstairs. At 2 a.m., we went to her room to check on her. Her temp had now dropped a signal of impending delivery, but she wanted to play ball! We were torn. Is she not in whelp, and do we call it a night and go home? Or stay there and wear ourselves out more on the chance that she would deliver soon. We decided that it was too risky to drive the forty-five miles back home and decided to get a hotel room a block away and monitor her from there, while trying to get a little sleep. I couldn't sleep. I feared that the first pup was going to be an affected male and she wouldn't know what to do, resulting in him dying. Three a.m.— nothing. Four a.m.— nothing. Five-thirty a.m., a dark thing in the box. We ran to check on what was happening, and my worst fear had come true, a deceased male pup. He was followed by four female pups. My heart sank with the delivery of each female. I figured we had at best four carrier females. This would be my first litter without an affected pup.

Just prior to the birth of that litter, Voodoo came into season. I asked Casey if we should even try using the *revived* frozen Rocky semen, but he didn't see the point. Our usual semen donor had sold his stud dog, so I was in a scramble to get another stud dog lined up. While discussing my situation with one of the other techs, she mentioned a guy who worked in another lab that had beagles. We went to talk to him, and he graciously offered up the use of either of his two beagles. My prayers were answered…, without a second to lose.

Voodoo was bred on a Friday during the middle of an ice storm. After the breeding, Kristin and I were driving home and she checked her e-mail. Brandon, the tech at Harvard that does the genotyping for us, gave us the absolute best news I have ever received: We had THREE affected females and one carrier in Elvira's litter! We did it; we made history! Kristin called Alison, who hadn't seen the email yet, and they cried happy tears on the phone. I called Casey but got voicemail. While I was calling him, he was calling me to tell me the news and to say use Rocky again! I dropped Kristin off at her home and cried the entire drive to my house. This was one of the proudest moments of my career.

Sunday, we once again made the forty-five-mile drive to breed Voodoo to frozen Rocky semen. Everything went smoothly and once again the wait was on.

Meanwhile, we had to relocate the affected puppies from Winston-Salem, NC to Dr. Childers in Seattle, WA. This was a huge challenge as these were the very first affected female MTM dogs. We had no idea of how stable they were, how long they would remain stable, and how well they would handle stress. A cross country move on a normal pup would be challenging, but for these girls, unimaginable. Once again, Alison decided to take responsibility and see that these fragile babies were to receive the best of care. She refused to let them be shipped by a contracted carrier. Alison understood the importance of these puppies and especially this litter. She went to work and had WAKE agree to sign the puppies into her care to make the transport. She also asked if Kristen, Paul, and I would make this trek across the country with her and the pups. What an adventurous trip it was, and we made it! We survived the journey and now we must hand over the pups to the new institution. Not only am I seeing my job slowly slip away, but I'm also not going to be able to follow these pups on their adventure. Which treatment will they receive? Will they progress the same as the males? Will they thrive with treatment as Rocky, Turing, and Pavlov did? I had so many questions and so much sadness that I would not be a part of their life and story.

The following day, we were allowed to visit the rest of the colony. Just thinking about that day brings tears to my eyes. We were taken into the first room where we met Black and Orange. They looked fabulous. They were happy and still had their quirky personalities as they did back in North Carolina. There was another dog with a litter of pups…, and sadly, I can't remember who she was because I was looking at the two dogs in the back, right cage. They were too big to be the other females we shipped, but they didn't look like Pink and Blue. Then it dawned on me. That's Pavlov and Turing! These dogs looked like normal dogs. They were jumping and barking and flat out crazy. With Rocky, you could tell he was disabled, but not these two. I was overjoyed to see the girls, but absolutely amazed to look at Pavlov and Turing. In nearly fifteen years of working in the research field, I have never seen anything that amazing, and I'm not likely to ever see it again.

We left that room to go to the *playroom*, a large area with an obstacle course for the dogs to enjoy. We went there to meet Pink, Blue, Black, and Orange. We played with them two at a time, and I was so pleased to see that they loved their new people and seemed to have settled into life in Washington. Finally, it was time to bring out Pavlov and Turing. Once again, I was filled with an overwhelming sense of astonishment. Not only did those two look normal, but they were very agile, jumping on and off of the tables. Never did I expect them to be in this good of condition. It's hard to put into words my wonder and incredulity while looking at Pavlov and Turing. If gene therapy can do this for dogs, what can it do for humans? I, for one, can't wait to find out.

A few weeks later, back in North Carolina, Voodoo's litter was born— three boys and two females. This would be my last MTM litter and possibly a very special one if any of those pups were Rocky's. Generally, when a pup is born, it is microchipped, dew claws are removed, and a cheek swab is taken and sent to Brandon. Within a few days he sends me the results. As luck would be, Brandon had issues with the assay, and these results took an excruciatingly long two weeks to come back. After what felt like an eternity, I received an email from Brandon: "Sorry for the delay... however, I'm seeing Homozygous affected females...?"

This was the absolute best news I have ever received and beyond worth the wait. It was truly the proudest moment of my life. We brought Rocky back to life!

MTM will forever be a part of my life. Even now, after all the dogs have left, I can't help but be excited to read articles on the development of the research. I have connected with MTM families and feel their hurt, their joys, and their hope that someday their children will get to experience what I have seen with these dogs. Every dog that I touched has a special place in my heart. They have paved the way for great things to come.

81

CHAPTER 17

EXCERPTS FROM THE MUSCLE DREAM TEAM

Letters From the Doctors

Anthony Atala, MD, is the Director of the Wake Forest Institute for Regenerative Medicine, and the W. Boyce Professor and Chair of Urology at Wake Forest University.

The story of Joshua Frase is actually a story about the entire Frase family. During my career as a pediatric surgeon, I have met many families who face difficult health challenges with grace and courage. But the Frases stand out. Not only did they provide an environment that gave their son the strength and determination to reach for the stars; they formed a foundation to increase research into the neuro-muscular disease that affected Joshua and other children. The foundation is a family endeavor that has made a lasting impact on what we know about myotubular myopathy and how to potentially treat it.

My involvement with the Frase family started in 1997. We had just published one of our initial papers on the engineering of the first organ, and the article had been highlighted by the scientific journal to the media. My office received a message from a Mrs. Elsie Rockett. She left word that she had heard of our recently published work and wanted to speak to me. I called back and met Joshua's grandmother (Alison Frase's mother), by phone. I first learned about Joshua and his condition, myotubular myopathy (MTM), through my initial phone call with Elsie and Alison. I was asked if I could help by doing research that one day may benefit patients with MTM. I had no idea if I could, and a quick overview of the literature made me realize that there was almost no research being done for this condition to speak of. But I knew that research for MTM was important to Elsie, and, of course, to Joshua. I had plenty on my plate in terms of research that I needed to continue in the field of organ regeneration, but I could not take my mind off that phone call. I felt there was something that could be done. A subsequent phone call with Paul and Alison Frase convinced me this was something I had to do.

I was working at Children's Hospital and Harvard Medical School at the time, and I felt it was important to assemble a good research team. I contacted Lou Kunkel. His research laboratory was just a few floors below mine. Lou was well known for his discovery of the muscular dystrophy disease gene. This had been a major accomplishment in the field, as one of the very first genetic disorder genes to be identified and generated. Muscular dystrophy disease, like MTM, affected muscle tissues, but it was caused by another gene defect. Lou had not really worked with MTM, but he was working on gene therapy strategies, and he was equally intrigued with my proposal. Lou suggested that I also connect with Alan Beggs, another scientist in his department who was doing genetic analyses in patients with a variety of muscular disorders. Alan was excited about the possibilities. I felt we had assembled an excellent team, one that would combine our tissue regeneration strategies with gene therapy and molecular genetic strategies. Our "Dream Team" was ready to go. I could not wait to let Elsie and the Frases know that we were all committed to work on MTM. The first fundraiser was held and off we went pursuing research that could potentially be of help to Joshua and the other children with this devastating disease, MTM.

In January 2004, our research group moved from Boston to Winston Salem, North Carolina, to start the Wake Forest Institute for Regenerative Medicine at Wake Forest University. I called the Frases to let them know that despite our move, we were committed to see this work through. We continued our collaborations with the team in Boston. Shortly after arriving at Wake Forest, I helped to recruit a physical rehabilitation physician who would do his clinical work in the Department of Neurology, but who would also do his research work at our institute, Dr. Martin (Casey) Childers. He had been working with an animal colony of dogs with muscular dystrophy disease. The potential connection with MTM was not lost on us. I was hoping to recruit him into working with MTM as well. Once Casey began working at our institute, I introduced him to the work we were doing with MTM in the area of tissue regeneration, and I felt he would be the ideal person to bring this research forward into a large animal model, as this was his area of expertise. Through two separate phone calls on the same day, I was able to introduce Casey to the Frases, and we had a conversation with Alan Beggs. I could not have been happier, knowing that the work could continue into larger animals, and the work could evolve further with new therapies.

In the meantime, Joshua grew into an amazing young man who didn't focus on what he couldn't do—instead he made the most of what he could do. He was brave, compassionate, funny, and intelligent. He excelled at academics and dreamed of becoming a research scientist so he could find a cure for myotubular myopathy. I will never forget the day that Joshua visited us at our institute at Wake Forest. He was only a junior high school student, but he asked all sorts of insightful questions, and he had a scientific knowledge far superior than many college students I have known. He asked if one day he could work with us. I told him we would hold a spot open for him, and I meant it!

In addition to raising this remarkable young man, the Frases started a foundation from the ground up with the goal to cure Joshua and other children. In working with Paul and Alison, it is easy to see where Joshua got his optimism, commitment, and determination. Raising research funds for a little-known disease is a daunting task. At the time the foundation was started, there were only about fifty boys in the world known to have myotubular myopathy. But, like Joshua, his parents didn't focus on the difficulties and challenges. Instead, they dove in, raised funds, and helped to build a coalition of scientists from around the world. And it's important to note that the Frases' role extends beyond fund-raising. Through their networking and activism, they were able to locate a dog with myotubular myopathy, a significant finding that has changed the scope of research. Today, thanks to this advance, an international team is evaluating a promising gene therapy for myotubular myopathy.

As a researcher, it is an honor and a privilege to work in the field of regenerative medicine because of its potential to impact patients' lives. With this focus on new therapies, our minds and hearts are always on the patients who need our help. For many years, Joshua was able to defy the odds and accomplish things that were seemingly impossible. Patients like Joshua inspire us. But, I must admit, we also have a huge sense of responsibility. We want very much to make rapid advances for the patients who are waiting, but it isn't always possible. Science sometimes moves in measured steps when we want very much to make giant leaps.

I wish with all of me that we had been able to find a cure for Joshua. But, like the Frases, our research team is carrying on its work in his memory. Joshua's life, so richly lived, continues to inspire us. While he didn't get the opportunity to do actual research, his dream is still alive. When researchers are able to find a treatment that can help patients like him, it will be Joshua's and his family's legacy.

Joshua had been inducted into the National Honor Society shortly before his death. If Joshua had been able to fulfill his dream of going into science, I have no doubt he would have made major contributions. Joshua was not able to come and work at our institute as he had wished. The spot we had left open for him to work at our institute will go unfilled. But personally, I will always keep a spot open for him—in my heart.

***

Alan H. Beggs, PhD, is the Director of The Manton Center for Orphan Disease Research at Boston Children's Hospital, and Sir Edwin and Lady Manton Professor of Pediatrics at Harvard Medical School.

Most PhD laboratory scientists never get a chance to see the impact their research has on real people. We spend our days working with little tubes of chemicals and solutions, or with mice, or cells in a dish. Sometimes we work with big tables of numbers containing hundreds of columns and thousands of rows. Always, our goal is to increase our understanding of God's glorious creation with the hope that we can improve our existence here on Earth. Rarely do we get to actually see that in action.

Joshua Miles Frase, and too many other children like him, have blessed me with this opportunity. Watching Joshua grow and inspire others, inspired me, and gave all of us motivation to do what we do. The progress sometimes seemed excruciatingly slow, and at other times, looking back since I first met Alison and Paul, I see how far we have come. Always, the goal has been the same—to improve the lives of all the Joshuas of the world through a better understanding of their conditions, and through developing effective treatments, and hopefully, one day, cures.

We stand now on the edge of success, with many new tools and the knowledge necessary to apply them in what have been the very first clinical trials to test treatments for X-linked myotubular myopathy ("XLMTM"). The path we followed was forged using the latest advances in genetics and medicine, and in so doing we created a scientific road map for how to attack many genetic conditions like Joshua's. This map is part of Joshua's legacy to all of us.

When Joshua was born in February of 1995, his scientific map was a blank. Terra incognito. Filled with unknowns. But even before his birth, Alison and Paul knew Joshua would be a special child. His growth in the womb was slower than expected, and his movements were weaker and less frequent than they should have been.

As soon as he was born, it was apparent that something wasn't quite right, as he immediately turned blue and had trouble breathing on his own. But once a breathing tube was inserted, Joshua turned a bright healthy pink and his heartbeat strongly within him. His muscles, however, were weak, with no tone and he had no gag reflex and a weak suck—quite unlike what one might expect for the son of an NFL lineman!

For our muscles to operate properly, we need to initiate and coordinate their contractions with our brains, and then the signals need to travel down our spinal cords to our nerves, the wiring system of our bodies. Finally, those signals reach our muscles, which themselves are complex machines with a finely tuned collection of proteins arranged in repeated arrays of contractile units. If any one of these steps of the process is impaired, then the muscles won't contract properly. Thus, the "disease map" for a weak infant includes different continents for the brain and spinal cord, for the nerves, and for the muscles themselves. The first task then, when a child is born weak, is to determine where the problem lies.

The cause of Joshua's weakness was a mystery, but the early indications suggested a possible problem with the nerves in his spinal cord, or in his muscles themselves. Usually, for the first few weeks or months of life, the doctors are most concerned with stabilizing the child and with conducting less invasive tests in hopes of finding out what's going on. Joshua's case was typical, as all the initial tests came back inconclusive until he was three and a half months old when a muscle biopsy was done. This allows the doctors to examine the muscle under the microscope to determine its structure and is an essential step in diagnosing a group of conditions called *congenital myopathies*. *Congenital myopathy* is a term given to a group of muscle ("myo") diseases ("pathy") that are typically present at birth ("congenital"). What the doctors saw in Joshua's muscle were muscle fibers that were variable in size, with many much smaller than expected, and with the nuclei positioned in the center of the muscle cells instead of at the edges where they should have been. This pattern had been seen before, but had only been reported in the medical literature for the first time in 1966 when I, and Joshua's parents, were infants and children ourselves. Called "myotubular myopathy", or "MTM", because the small muscle fibers with central nuclei resembled *myotubes*, which are a normal stage of fetal muscle development; the cause was a mystery, but early studies had shown a genetic basis for this. The condition was found to run in families, often being passed on to affected sons by unaffected or *carrier* mothers. This inheritance pattern is characteristic of genes on the X chromosome, hence the *X-linked* in XLMTM. Since all women and girls have two X chromosomes, they can carry one with an abnormal gene yet still be unaffected because of the presence of one "good" copy on the second X. But when the chromosome with the abnormal gene is inherited by a son, who gets a Y chromosome from his father, there is no good copy to compensate. Thus, Joshua's disease map was taking shape— his weakness was due to a defect in his muscles, and that defect was caused by a gene on the X chromosome.

Often called "orphan diseases" because they are so rare that there is little commercial or academic interest in studying them, disorders like XLMTM, which is estimated to afflict roughly 1 in 50,000 boys, are understudied, and traditionally, little progress has been made in finding treatments or cures. A few years before Joshua was born, scientists in

87

Europe had mapped the gene for XLMTM to a particular part of the X chromosome, but little more was known about what it was or what it did. However, advances in genetic technology were occurring rapidly. Remarkably, just one year after Joshua's birth, in June 1996, Dr. Jocelyn Laporte and his colleagues in Strasbourg, France, working with collaborators in Germany and Sweden, discovered the XLMTM gene, called "MTM1", and named the protein it encoded *myotubularin* after the disease that its defect caused. This advance allowed many children like Joshua, whose diagnosis was based only on what his muscle looked like under the microscope, to have genetic testing to confirm the exact cause of his weakness, and it also provided opportunities for genetic counseling and family planning for their families. Within a year, Joshua entered into one of the very first research studies to examine the MTM1 gene in a large group of boys with XLMTM. His mutation was found and discovered to be a simple change of an amino acid, arginine (R) at position 69 of the myotubularin protein, into another amino acid, cysteine (C), hence it is designated *R69C*. This very same change has been seen in other boys with XLMTM and has been associated with varying degrees of severity among these children. Thus, by the end of 1997, Joshua's map had become very much clearer—we knew that he carried a mutation of the MTM1 gene that altered a protein called myotubularin, and the result was a defect in his muscles that weakened them and inhibited their contraction.

So what was this defect, and why didn't Joshua's muscles contract properly? When it was first discovered, the sequence of myotubularin was shown to be similar to other previously studied *phosphatase* enzymes, which are a specialized type of proteins that catalyze chemical reactions in our cells. Phosphatases have the special ability to remove a phosphate group from other proteins or lipids (fats), and this simple chemical change can have profound effects on the functions of those protein or lipids, sometimes turning their activity on or off, or changing their identity so they function differently in our cells. Myotubularin was soon shown to act on lipids, and in simple model systems, such as yeast, these lipids were shown to be important for marking certain membranes within the cell. By so doing, they created molecular *signposts* or address labels, designating, for example, one membrane as belonging to a vesicle called an *endosome*, which the cell used to take up nutrients from the outside.

These advances provided the first clues, but still didn't explain why the muscles of boys like Joshua were so weak. The next hint came from studies we did in collaboration with Dr. Anna Buj-Bello, in France, which revealed the exact location of myotubularin within muscle. It turned out that myotubularin was found at special membrane structures called *sarcoplasmic reticulum* (SR), where we now believe it plays a role in controlling the lipid content, and hence structure, of the membranes. As it turns out, the SR is critical for muscle function. When a nerve impulse reaches the muscle, it results in a flood of calcium ions rushing out from the SR, and this increase in calcium inside the muscle is what triggers contraction. When the SR in muscles from boys like Joshua was examined, it was found to be misshapen, and sometimes missing, explaining at least in part why the muscle was unable to contract properly.

Knowing that defective calcium entry into muscle causes weakness in XLMTM was an important advance because it suggested that searching for drugs that improve calcium influx might lead to new treatments. However, it was clear that the SR calcium release defect was not the only thing going on. Many proteins, including myotubularin, perform several different functions within the cell, and understanding all these functions was going to be important if we ever hoped to treat the entire disease. This is where the research participation of boys like Joshua and their families becomes so important, because when they give permission for scientists to study their DNA and muscle biopsies, we can examine the muscle directly for more abnormalities.

To make a long story short, a series of studies that we, and our collaborators and colleagues around the world, have done has recently led to a new appreciation for the diversity of disease mechanisms leading to weakness in XLMTM. We now understand that myotubularin does more than just help create healthy and functional SR. It also binds to part of the cell's skeleton, *the cytoskeleton*, where it helps control the shape and position of cellular components such as the nuclei that appear to get stuck in the centers of the muscle fibers. There is some evidence that lack of myotubularin causes abnormalities of mitochondria, the so-called powerhouses of the cell that create ATP— the chemical form of energy necessary for life. Finally, it may also regulate the membranes at the neuromuscular junctions where the nerve impulses are transferred over to the muscle. Already, this information is being used in early-stage clinical tests of a drug that improves neuromuscular transmission. Without question, knowing the lay of the land of these new pieces of the scientific map will be critical in the coming years to guiding the development of additional new treatments, and assessing whether they are effective.

Examining the genes, proteins, and muscles of all the Joshuas generous and brave enough to participate in the research studies has been essential. Without this help, none of the scientific progress described above would have been possible. However, there are limits to what can be done with children, so the other key ingredient is the availability of faithful animal models to study and test new treatments with. Since evolution has used and re-used many of the same building blocks over and over again, we find, for example, that the myotubularin gene is present, with much the same functions, in many other species ranging from mammals, to fish, and even down to single cell organisms like yeast!

Obviously, yeast have no muscles, so studying myotubularin there has limited benefit for learning why Joshua's muscles were weak, but there are methods now to create targeted mutations of a gene in many species including mice, and even in zebrafish, like the ones sold in pet stores. In 2002, Anna Buj-Bello published a paper describing how she developed a strain of myotubularin *knock-out* (KO) mice, in which the Mtm1 gene was mutated or "KO'd", leading to severe muscle weakness. The symbols for mouse genes are the same as for human ones but use lowercase letters after the first one. Examination of their muscles under the microscope showed that the affected mice had many of the same abnormalities as seen in children with XLMTM, and because mice have a shorter natural life span, and cannot be treated with the same degree of support that children receive, the disease in these animals was rapidly fatal, with affected mice surviving for only a couple of months. This turned out to be a boon for studies designed to test treatments that might be effective over short periods of time, because they could be done relatively rapidly, but it also made it harder to test the long-term effects of partial treatments over time spans more similar to human patients. To address this problem, we developed a second, milder mouse model that makes an abnormal, partially functional, form of myotubularin, as opposed to making none at all. In fact, we chose to create the exact same R69C mutation in the Mtm1 gene that had been found in Joshua and a number of other children with milder, and more variable forms of XLMTM. These mice survive for well over a year but exhibit many of the characteristic muscle defects and weakness of XLMTM, making them also a good system to test new therapies. The availability of faithful animal models is another key step in the march toward developing treatments, and represents the discovery of an entire new country to explore in our scientific map of XLMTM.

All the studies of the MTM1 gene that had been done on DNA and muscle samples from Josh and other children with XLMTM had shown us that the underlying cause of this disease was either complete absence of myotubularin, or presence of an altered and less functional version of the protein. Thus, XLMTM is caused by deficiency of myotubularin. In theory then, an effective targeted therapy would be any treatment that provides normal myotubularin protein back to the sick muscles. *Gene replacement therapy* is just such an approach. In one form of gene therapy, an unmutated *good* or therapeutic copy of a gene is inserted into cells of a sick individual who suffers from the effects of carrying only *bad* or mutant copies of that same gene. The hope and expectation is that this therapeutic gene will be carried in the patient's cells where it will be turned on and direct the production of functional copies of the missing or defective protein. To do this, we require a delivery vehicle, called a *vector*, to introduce that therapeutic gene into the living cells of the recipient. It turns out that viruses are masters of doing exactly that as they normally infect cells by injecting copies of their own DNA and hijacking the cellular machinery to replicate those DNA molecules as well as reading the instructions of the viral DNA to make viral proteins to produce more viruses. Thus, one of the most effective methods for gene therapy that has been developed in recent years is to hijack the hijackers! Scientists have engineered special viral vectors in which the genes for viral replication and production are removed, leaving a spot to insert their favorite therapeutic gene. The hybrid DNA molecules are then packaged up with all the normal viral proteins to create an infectious particle, or delivery vehicle, that is capable of attaching to a cell and injecting the therapeutic gene carried within.

With this plan in mind, Anna Buj-Bello, working at the French institute Généthon outside of Paris, led an international team, which I was privileged to be part of, in a project to develop a viral vector called "AAV", carrying a normal copy of the myotubularin gene. When Anna injected this vector into a single leg muscle of her Mtm1 KO mice, those muscles grew larger and stronger, and when they were examined under the microscope, many of the characteristic abnormalities were corrected! Very importantly, as predicted, the treated muscles now contained myotubularin, which had been previously absent. This proof of concept demonstrated that replacing myotubularin, even in muscle that was already formed and developing weakness, was an effective approach to treating XLMTM. In a parallel series of studies using these same mice, my laboratory has partnered with a small biotechnology company called 4s3 Biosciences to develop an alternative approach called *protein replacement therapy* where the actual missing protein itself is delivered to the muscle. Both these methods, gene therapy and protein replacement therapy, have tremendous promise, and I can now envision a day when children like Joshua may receive either one or the other of these, or perhaps a combination of these two treatments to build and restore their muscles.

Studies in mice are all well and good, and often are the first step toward eventual clinical trials in humans but testing just a single muscle in such a small animal is still a far cry from treating children like Joshua. I recall discussing with Alison the importance of having a larger animal model, more similar in size and physiology to human children, with which to test potential new treatments for XLMTM. Miraculously, within a year of that discussion, I was contacted by a good friend and colleague, Dr. Diane Shelton, who is a veterinary pathologist at the University of California at San Diego who specializes in diagnosing neuromuscular diseases in dogs and cats. Diane told me that she had examined the muscles from a group of Labrador retrievers referred to her by some veterinarian colleagues in Saskatchewan, Canada. The vets reported that these dogs developed a progressive and rapidly fatal weakness over the first six months of life. Both the clinical findings and appearance of the muscle under the microscope, were similar to what was seen in children with XLMTM. Based on their urging, both Jocelyn Laporte's group and my own sequenced the affected dog's myotubularin genes, finding a mutation much like the ones seen in human patients. To seal the deal, when we examined the myotubularin protein, it too was abnormal, convincing us that these dogs had exactly the same disease as Joshua!

Now the dilemma was to decide the best way that these dogs could help us to understand and treat XLMTM. All the dogs treated by the vets in Canada had died, but one of their female siblings named Nibs, was alive and well and living on a farm outside of Saskatchewan. Although all the doctors were skeptical, Alison was determined to make a connection with Nibs' owner to ask whether he would allow her to help in the quest to find a cure for XLMTM. In a series of extraordinary events that are certainly unique in my experience as a scientist and medical researcher, Alison single-handedly flew out to Saskatchewan, and retrieved a chocolate brown Labrador that possibly carried the gene responsible for MTM. There are more details of this amazing story, from Alison's perspective, in Chapter 16. As two mothers who both carried mutated copies of the XLMTM gene, Alison and Nibs established an immediate bond. All it took was a mother's "vision, fortitude, and resolve (Alison's motto) to demonstrate the desperate need, and explain the path forward. In a remarkable act of generosity, Nibs' owner donated her to the Joshua Frase Foundation. Within days, Alison was flying back to Jacksonville with Nibs at her side to start a colony of dogs that would lead the way to developing a treatment for XLMTM.

Just a few years earlier, Dr. Martin ("Casey") Childers had joined the Institute for Regenerative Medicine at Wake Forrest University, where the Frase Foundation had already been supporting research on XLMTM. Casey had previously studied golden retrievers with a form of muscular dystrophy and knew exactly how powerfully useful the dogs could be. With the help of an enormous and highly skilled team of veterinarians and animal care experts at Wake Forrest, Casey took Nibs into his own home and bred her to start a colony of dogs carrying the myotubularin mutation (there is more about this in his section later in this chapter, and in Chapter 16). The successful demonstration that a single dose of gene therapy corrects the weakness in Nibs' descendants with XLMTM led to the creation of a new biotechnology company that dedicated its first project to developing this treatment for the Joshuas of the world. Begun in September of 2017, the first trial of MTM1 gene therapy for XLMTM has shown tremendous promise, with many treated boys able to reduce or eliminate the breathing support they needed, and achieving new milestones such as sitting up, standing, and even taking their first steps. Although still in an early phase, we are hopeful and excited that this will just be the first of several effective therapies for XLMTM to be approved for use to treat this deadly condition.

So now, Joshua's scientific map has taken its final shape. The defective gene for XLMTM (MTM1) is known. The protein encoded by this gene, myotubularin, has been studied, and its role in proper muscle function is beginning to be understood. Faithful animal models of XLMTM have been developed and discovered and were used to test and demonstrate the effectiveness of a potential new treatment. With this information, we were able to map out the road to developing treatments. We knew which gene to correct, which protein to replace, and how to test the safety and effectiveness of these treatments before planning the first human trial. With the expertise and resources of the biotechnology industry, these advances are being translated into what we hope will be a safe and effective treatment that can be applied in the clinic.

Today, there is unprecedented activity and excitement among the scientific, medical, commercial, and patient communities, with hope not just for the imminent approval of a gene therapy, but also a variety of other methods to treat XLMTM under development by other academic and commercial scientists. These advances were only possible because of a three-way partnership between academic laboratories, biotechnology, and pharmaceutical companies, and an active and engaged patient and family community. The Joshua Frase Foundation, with the passionate leadership of Joshua's parents, Alison and Paul, along with a number of other independent and cooperating patient advocacy groups, has been a catalyst for much of this, stimulating interest, educating and informing patients and their families, raising critical funding, and establishing partnerships with numerous other organizations such as the Muscular Dystrophy Association of the USA, Généthon (in France), the Congenital Muscle Disease

International Registry, and more. They say, "It takes a community," and that couldn't be more true than here. By reminding us all that it's about the children, Joshua and all the kids like him have inspired an amazing international group of collaborators to come together to work for this common goal.

As I sat there at Joshua's funeral in 2010 listening to the incredible outpouring of love and support, I remember feeling that his passing represented one of the greatest failures of my professional life. But slowly, I realized that in fact we were celebrating a spectacular success. Listening to all the people whose lives Joshua touched, whose experiences he enriched, and whose passions and careers he inspired, I realized that he gave an incredible gift to us all. The road map that we developed in our quest to help all the Joshuas of the world provides not just directions for finding a cure for XLMTM, but also a map to follow for other orphan diseases that have yet to be tackled. That is surely a tremendous legacy to leave!

***

Martin K. (Casey) Childers D.O., Ph.D., serves as the Chief Medical Officer for Asklepios Biopharmaceutical, Inc., and was formerly a professor of medicine at the University of Washington.

Myotubular myopathy is both a rare and devastating disease of young children. Most do not survive beyond the second year of life. For that reason, and probably because of the lack of available genetic testing for those that survive, I had never seen a case of MTM in 24 years of clinical practice as an adult neuromuscular specialist. When the opportunity arose to become involved in developing the first dog colony for this disease, it was a steep learning curve, particularly given the lack of information in the literature about comparative animal models. We really did not know what to expect to find if such a colony could be established, nor was there a road map to begin to understand what to expect if we were to attempt to repeat Anna's gene therapy treatment of the MTM mice. We were starting with a clean slate. Fortunately, the world's top minds were gathered in the right place at the right time, and the team communicated and collaborated together. For me, it was the single most meaningful opportunity of my career as a clinician scientist and it was such a thrill to play a role in the "Dream Team" established by the Frase family.

At the time that Alison delivered to our family the chocolate Labrador retriever, "Nibs," who became the matriarch of the MTM dog colony, no one had successfully infused a gene therapy into all of the muscles of an animal (or a human). In fact, at that time, the most promising methods appeared to be infusing gene therapy into individual limbs under high pressure to force the experimental medicine into the muscular tissues. The problem, of course, is that the heart and the parachute-shaped diaphragm muscle cannot be infused in this manner. It didn't occur to us at the time that Anna's group had already demonstrated in her mice that this process was not necessary, that the genetic medicine developed by the team at Genethon was poised and ready to go, using a simple infusion into a leg vein. The simple intravenous infusion method had been attempted in other animal models and repeatedly failed, and we thought that although it worked in mice, this method was simply not going to work in large animals or humans.

The problem with whole body gene delivery in a large animal was only part of the challenge. Other issues seemed even more troublesome. We needed massive quantities of viral vectors to be able to understand the doses needed to advance the treatment. At that time, there were few, if any, viral vector cores that could undertake and fund such large quantities. Using methods available in most academic laboratories, generating enough vector to infuse the entire body of a single twenty-gram mouse was a big deal. Scaling this up a thousand-fold or more for a five-kilogram puppy was almost unthinkable. This required advanced methods for scaling of clinical products using large bioreactors and requiring millions of dollars to assemble the equipment and construct the special clean laboratory rooms capable of handling these resources.

In my mind, we faced an even greater challenge. How would we find all the resources required for a new canine animal colony? Feeding, housing, and caring for these growing puppies was not only expensive, but required specially trained and caring animal technicians, veterinarians, and staff. At

Wake Forest University, a dog colony had never been attempted. Dogs require specially designed housing with raised floors, an extraordinary amount of space to live and play, and they required daily intense human contact. These were all requirements specified by the USDA for the humane care of laboratory animals.

Despite the challenges of the scientific hurdles and lack of available resources, somehow the challenges were overcome and sufficient monies were raised at the just the right time when the resources were needed as described in the various chapters of this book. But the linchpin that enabled the dog discoveries came from the determination of Alison Frase. Alison brought the team together, found and delivered Nibs to the institute, and consistently encouraged us to work together with her words and by raising funds to get things started. Without her, we would not have had this remarkable medicine. Although it would have been tested in mice, at the time no one would invest in an experimental medicine for whole-body gene delivery to muscles without a convincing large animal model. A great example of this is in the book, *The Forever Fix*, where a young boy named Corey Haas is treated with a genetic medicine that results in a cure for blindness. Because the investigator had a remarkable dog model of genetic blindness, they were able to develop and test a genetic medicine in dogs and translate the findings to human patients with assurance.

One afternoon during the early years of the work at Wake Forest, the Frases came by the laboratory to introduce Joshua. It was just for a few minutes. He was fourteen or fifteen years old— about a year before he passed away. He couldn't move. He couldn't talk—he could only whisper, and I had a hard time understanding what he was saying. That was actually my first experience with a child with this rare disease and it really shocked me. The first opportunity to meet other patients came during a family conference—about thirty families with children with this myotubular myopathy. At that conference and after visiting with these families, I began to understand that Joshua had lived a remarkable life as sick as he was. That was really due to Paul and Alison's great medical care. He couldn't move. He could breathe with the aid of a positive pressure ventilator. I remember, after meeting Joshua, I was stunned. I went up to my office and sat there and looked out the window. The effects of the disease in patients were worse than I had expected. At the time, we had a promising treatment for MTM and we had an incredible model of the disease, thanks to Alison. What we really lacked was money to advance the treatment.

The grandchildren of Nibs gave us the opportunity to test and develop a systemic gene therapy for myotubular myopathy. We started by giving small doses (intramuscular injections) to three affected male puppies, and within three weeks, their muscles had increased in strength. The muscle was nearly normal. There were no signs of toxicity in the dogs, similar to the lack of toxicity in mice. MTM Mice live 62 days without any treatment, whereas treated mice survived up on two years of age with no signs of disease.

Eventually, we discovered that a single intravenous infusion of a genetic medicine, a viral vector (AAV) carrying a healthy copy of the MTM gene can completely restore normal health to dogs with a canine version of myotubular myopathy. This discovery, started with Alison's dedication, came about through the tireless work of scientists like Alan Beggs, Anna Buj-Bello, and many others working together to find a cure for a rare and devastating disease.

***

David L. Mack, PhD, is an Associate Professor of Rehabilitation Medicine, Bioengineering, Physiology and Biophysics for the Institute for Stem Cell and Regenerative Medicine at the University of Washington.

I remember with profound gratitude the day Casey recruited me to work on the MTM gene therapy dog project. Dr. Steve Walker and I were in a local Winston-Salem café, just down the street from WFIRM, when Casey walked by to grab a coffee. Steve instantaneously had an epiphany and blurted out that Casey and I should get to know each other because of our complementary but non-overlapping areas of expertise. I had been at WFIRM for more than a year and knew a little bit about Casey's research program from various internal seminars, but we remained siloed as scientists often do. Casey was a physician who cared for patients with neuromuscular diseases, while I'm a geneticist and developmental biologist more focused on the molecular causes of disease. Casey's group had just shown that regional hindlimb perfusion of AAV-MTM1 into Pavlov and Turing's (two of the dogs) failing muscles restored strength to almost normal levels in a matter of weeks. As the gene therapy program embarked on a path toward eventual FDA approval, it needed to include a new facet to explain WHY and HOW gene transfer worked at the molecular level—similar to what had been shown in Anna's and Alan's MTM KO and R69C mutant mouse experiments. I didn't realize at the time, but this initial conversation with Casey would put my career on a new trajectory and give me the opportunity to contribute to the most rewarding collaboration of my professional life.

It's enormously exciting when any research scientist generates strong evidence that a revolutionary therapy has the potential to improve the lives of patients—especially if no alternatives are available and doubly so if those patients are children who will otherwise not survive. During this exciting window of time, the depth and breadth of future experiments that could and should be done expands dramatically, almost overnight. The excitement is counterbalanced by the burden of urgency, knowing that the MTM boys are *on the clock* from the day they're born. During most of 2012, Casey was running an international scientific collaboration, talking to biotech start-ups interested in our technology and starting to think about the clinical trial. He needed someone to take charge of the day-to-day experiments while he focused on the big picture. I enthusiastically filled that need, which eventually led to us moving the whole research program from WFIRM to the University of Washington as a team.

Pavlov and Turing, the two dogs treated with the MTM1 gene transfer vector that Anna had developed, adapted quickly and happily to their new home at UW. Untreated dogs carrying a mutation in their MTM1 gene normally die by 4-5 months of age from generalized muscle weakness and an inability to breath because of failing diaphragm. Just shy of their first birthday on moving day, they were the best pre-clinical proof so far that a vector-delivered MTM1 gene could be disseminated throughout the body and make enough myotubularin protein in the right place at the right time to restore muscle function. As a developmental biologist, this was astounding to me! That means during embryogenesis, while their muscles were being built from scratch, 99.999% of the muscle machinery was laid down perfectly. However, when it came time to build the sarcoplasmic reticulum (calcium handling lipid membrane networks), the muscle cytoskeleton that support organelles like mitochondria and parts of the neuromuscular junction, the muscle cells were missing an essential protein, myotubularin. At this point, multiple investigators had shown that muscles lacking myotubularin can't contract. For a summary, refer to the chapter by our colleague, Alan Beggs. What I found intriguing was that non-contractile, severely atrophied muscle could remain in a state of developmental arrest or quiescence—a sort of suspended animation—for months after birth. Pavlov and Turing were both treated at 10 weeks of age, when the myopathy was apparent but had not progressed too far. Upon receiving the normal MTM1 transgene delivered by the viral vector, the muscles simply plugged the normal myotubularin protein into all the right places and began to contract normally within weeks. To dramatically over-simplify, this seemed analogous to your car not starting because of defective spark plugs. Replace them and the car starts right up.

Since those heady days when the Frase's Dream Team demonstrated for the first time that a muscle disease could be corrected with gene transfer, Pavlov and Turing continue to be our superstars. A major question for the entire field of gene therapy is how long an AAV-mediated gene transfer will last. Clinical trials evaluating factor-IX gene transfer for hemophilia have shown durability out to a decade with minimal loss in plasma concentrations. But it's challenging and dangerous to apply what we've learned from one disease, target tissue (e.g. liver for hemophilia and muscle for MTM) and vector combination to other conditions. To answer the durability question for a congenital myopathy, we have continued to assess Pavlov and Turing on a yearly basis. Sometime around January every year, we reunite a subset of the Dream Team, including Rob Grange, Anna Buj-Bello, Mike Lawlor, and Jessica Snyder to evaluate the dogs' gait, neurological function, hindlimb strength and diaphragm/respiratory capacity. Tiny muscle biopsies are taken to measure the levels of remaining AAV vectors and myotubularin protein. Thin histological sections are cut to determine if or when the hallmarks of disease pathology (small muscle fibers, centrally located nuclei and mis localized mitochondria) might reemerge. The overarching goal is to record and correlate myotubularin protein levels to muscle strength and histological appearance over the years so the FDA can evaluate how well and how long the therapy will be effective. As of February 2022, nine years after receiving gene transfer, Pavlov and Turing continue to thrive with no loss of muscle strength and no signs of relapse. All evidence points to AAV-mediated gene transfer for a congenital myopathy lasting at least a decade. But a decade does not a life make. The best scenario will be to treat infants with MTM as early as possible, before secondary pathology caused by constant ventilator support, lack of movement, being fed through a feeding tube has complicated or detracted from the ultimate level of correction they might have achieved. Our next challenge as scientists is to figure out how to administer a second dose of gene therapy in these boys without setting off a firestorm of an immune reaction.

On the morning of February 2, 2022, while doing the year 9 post treatment assessments on Pavlov and Turing, I decided to share this picture of Pavlov with Alison and Paul over text messaging and tell them the good news. I pointed out that Pavlov was getting old, noting the grey hair around his eyes and muzzle. Who would have thought these dogs, which would have otherwise died around 4-5 months of age, would live and thrive this long. After the whooping and virtual back-slapping had subsided, Alison re-minded me that this day would have been Joshua's 27th birthday. Then they both reiterated a message that I had heard so often over the years, that there are no coincidences in this shared odyssey. Unfortunately, I never had the privilege of meeting Joshua—he passed away about a year before I joined Casey's team. But on this day, I felt connected to his enduring spirit and proud to be contributing to his legacy.

***

Kevin J. Sullivan, MD, works in the Department of Pediatrics Division of Pediatric Critical Care Medicine at Nemours Children's Specialty Care.

I've been at the place for thirteen years. It was the first job I had out of training and Joshua was one of the first patients I ever met when I came out of training. I felt a lot of responsibility for his safety. I was always struck early on by Alison and Paul's dedication to the child. When he would come in with the complication of his respiratory status, would he be able to fight? He had such muscle weakness—had great trouble fighting his way through colds. I remember distinctly the first couple of times we were having to make those decisions. Is it time to put the breathing tube in—most of the time we were able to get by without it. For me, Alison and Paul were among the first parents who were savvy consumers of health care. In most cases, parents of children with new, acute illnesses don't know what to do. They essentially taught me the skill of how to meet the families halfway; of the fact that some parents who had chronically ill children know best. They had a good feeling for Joshua's needs. From the physician side of it, we have to size up the situation—are these people who are in denial? They weren't reckless. The horns came unlocked quickly.

There are five or six doctors in ICU—on duty every fourth or fifth week—a twenty percent chance I'd see Joshua. It's a testament to the care they were able to provide for him at home that I didn't see him more often.

He was a very fragile child. I was always amazed at how skilled they were at being able to give him the care he needed. Joshua was the first one I met that had myotubular myopathy. The other thing I learned from Joshua was how he very stoically dealt with the cards life had dealt him. I felt sorry for him, being trapped in his body with an intact mind. I've grown up as a physician since we first met, and I've seen a lot of suffering, but what I always took from Joshua was his intelligence and spirit. One of the other things the Frase family taught me—I'm just an ICU physician. My job is not that hard…you have to stay up at night and guard the children, but by no means are we PhD research people like the ones that the Frase family and foundation helped. I did notice that there are different classes of people who deal with severe illness differently. The Frases are people who have the wherewithal and the intelligence to not settle for one physician. They have formed a pyramid of healthcare consumers with savvy education and resources. Often-times, they'll know much more about the disease than we will.

At the time we met, early on, we had just had our first and second child. You don't have an appreciation when you're not a parent. In retrospect, now with three teenage daughters of my own, knowing the love you have for your own children—to be dealt that hand in life is a hard road to walk. They had the grace for it.

I always remember, even when he couldn't breathe and even when he had the mask on his face—the BiPap—very weak arms and hands—there were these die-cast metal cars in his hands. Throughout the illness, he'd hold them in his hands, laying there quietly and holding his cars. This was a little boy who had all the little boy interests, and to be dealt a genetic disease like that—I always struggled with that.

Paul was a big guy with a lot of muscle mass—a strapping guy with long hair— it always struck me— the dichotomy of this very physically fit man carrying this boy— a protective presence over the child.

Now, thirteen years later, I've been diagnosed with rheumatoid arthritis. There are days I don't feel so good but I think back to children like Joshua. We all have our cross to bear. If an 8- or 9-year-old can bear up, so can I.

I tell the residents now—since that time—two things: 1) You don't have an appreciation for what those parents are going through unless you have your own children. You are charged with safeguarding their most precious possession; and 2) If you want to make a jackass of yourself, the best way to do that is to disregard what the parents tell you.

CHAPTER 18

CHERRY PICKING: THE NEW NORMAL

Paul

Josh was twelve years old. We were driving through a small country town in the hills of North Carolina called Ararat, a little northeast of Pilot Mountain, which is near the town where Andy Griffith grew up. We loved going there in the summertime to visit family friends.

That day, "Big Stu," as we all affectionately called Mr. Epperson, was taking us to do something he'd grown up doing over the years. Nestled in the hills of Ararat was Levering Orchard, an apple orchard founded by Frank Levering in 1908 and transformed into a cherry orchard by his son Sam in the 1970s. Big Stu wanted to take us cherry picking. I'd never been before, and all I knew of harvesting cherries was what I'd seen on TV when an arm on a massive machine would literally reach out and grab the trunk of the cherry tree while what looked like a satellite dish opened below the tree. The arm would begin to shake the tree violently, and the cherries would all fall into the waiting *dish* below.

We took a left turn onto the road that would lead us to the hillside. On the right was an old, dilapidated warehouse that looked like it had been abandoned years ago. I later learned that the warehouse was full of life for about three months out of the year, processing hundreds of tons of cherries and shipping them to distribution centers where they'd end up being sent all over the world.

After another few hundred yards, we broke through the heavily wooded area to a hillside that had a very steep grade. Strategically planted along the steep grade were hundreds of cherry trees. These trees were a bit smaller than I'd expected, and they were a different breed of cherries than I was familiar with. I'd always known of the dark red Bing Cherries, but these were Rainier Cherries, a yellow cherry that faded to a light red or dark orange in spots. We passed through this section of the orchard, and the hillside leveled off to a field filled with large cherry trees ranging from twenty to thirty feet tall. They were filled with cherries, and each tree had a tall wooden ladder that was shaped specifically for harvesting cherries from these trees by hand. At the base of the ladder, the rails were spread approximately four feet wide for stability, and they narrowed to about twelve inches at the top. The ladders were anywhere from twelve to twenty feet tall, and the narrow tops allowed you to maneuver the ladders amongst the tree branches as you placed the ladder against the trunk.

We parked the van and the cars, and everyone piled out of the vehicles. We all posed for a portrait which came out quite well with the beautiful hills of Virginia for a backdrop, and then the sprint to the top of the trees was on. I was in no hurry; I was going to stay with Joshua and meander through the trees to find a low branch for Joshua to pick from. At this point in his life, Joshua was weak to the point of having to be pulled around in a wagon. He was too weak to sit up in a wheelchair. We'd managed to outfit a plastic Radio Flyer wagon that I pulled Joshua around in everywhere we went. As with the hillside and blueberry picking nine years earlier, I'd make a way for Joshua to enjoy the experience of picking cherries. I'd give him a *normal* experience.

I needed to find a branch low enough that Joshua could reach and pick cherries. The smaller trees we'd passed earlier were too far down the hill to walk to. The type of cherry tree we stood in front of was massive compared to the Rainier trees. There were no low hanging branches from which to pick fruit. I couldn't even bend a smaller branch down to Joshua. His wagon, at about ten inches off the ground, prevented him from getting close to the cherries, so I was going to have to bring the cherries to Joshua. I pulled the wagon close to the base of a tree and started climbing the ladder so I could grab a branch loaded with cherries and hang one in front of Joshua. I could not find a small branch long enough to dangle, so I broke off a couple of branches that had plenty of cherries on them and climbed back down the ladder.

When I think about that day, I feel like it exemplified the times of my life with Josh when I was a good dad, because, quite frankly, I wasn't always a good dad. But, right then, I think I was the best. I wanted my son to experience everything, I wanted him to experience normal. If he could not go and grab ahold of life, I was going to grab it for him, bring it to him, and let him experience it for himself. Different than what a normal father with a *normal* son would do…, but…this was our *normal*. And I wouldn't change it for the world.

CHAPTER 19

JOSHUA AND BELLA: PLAY STATION FOLLIES

We were blessed that Joshua and Bella were like a normal brother and sister, regardless of Joshua's disability. On Saturday mornings, Bella wanted to be right in the middle of Joshua's business, no matter what he was doing.

One of Joshua's favorite pass times became PlayStation™. He played games from racing cars to Call of Duty, and Bella asked to play them all. But she was three years old, and big brothers don't have any time for little sisters to cramp their style. Bella would come into Joshua's room and beg and plead to play with him, but he vehemently denied her access to the second controller until Alison or I entered the room. After some cajoling, and the usual threat of lifelong banishment from PlayStation™, Joshua reluctantly agreed to let his sister play, directing me to the #2 controller out of four. He had four controllers for when his buddies came over to play, so we had to find the right controller that could function with only two players online. I found the correct controller and handed it to Bella who'd been patiently sitting on Joshua's bed, knowing that the sheriff and deputy had entered the room, and there would be justice on her behalf.

Joshua talked her through setting up her controller, and they began to play together. Obviously, Bella had no idea what she was doing, but I knew it was just a matter of time until she'd picked up the configuration of the controls and learned the objectives of the games. It would not be long before she was competing with Joshua and possibly beating him, although that would have been quite a feat. He was so good that he destroyed his friends when they came over to play against him. They were all very good, but he was better and proved it time and again.

As all calmed down, and Josh and Bella began to play nice with each other, I usually slipped out of the room to attend to my weekend honey-do list. From that point on, that's how we spent Saturday mornings. Alison and I would work around the house, and Joshua and Bella would play games in his room. I'd walk in from time to time over the next few months and watch as Isabella seemed to be getting the hang of the controls, reacting to things that took place on the screen. Joshua always got the better of her, but that was to be expected.

One Saturday morning, about a week after Joshua let Bella join him in his gaming, I heard Bella say in a loud voice, "Hey, Joshua, how come I can't move my player?"

Joshua mumbled, "I don't know, maybe the batteries are dead." Bella continued to bellow about her controller not working and that she couldn't move her player. I came in and checked the batteries and they were fine. I didn't see anything wrong with it, so I handed it back to Bella and stood there to watch as she tried to engage the player. Bella took the controls and proceeded to tap away at the buttons with no reaction.

Bella yelled, "Hey, wait a minute; this controller is not working! What the heck, Josh? This controller is not working!" I looked at Joshua and saw a slight smile cross his lips, and I heard a quiet chuckle under his breath. When Bella said, "Hey, this is not working, and it has never worked!" Joshua busted out laughing. He'd been caught. The scheme that had fooled all of us for the last week had been revealed; Joshua had never engaged Bella's controller, and she'd never been in control of her player. All this time, Bella thought she was playing Play-Station™ with her brother, but Joshua pulled a fast one on us all. Joshua began to laugh one of his laughs when he laughed so hard that he couldn't breathe, and then he'd have to stop and catch his breath. We all started laughing, especially Bella. Josh's con was up, and he was about to have to teach his sister how to play PlayStation™, this time for real.

About four years later, Bella gave Josh a little payback.

It was a Saturday morning about 8 a.m., and I heard Joshua yelling at the top of his lungs. "Dad, Dad, come here! Dad, come here, PLEASE!" It sounded urgent, but Joshua was not panicked, and besides, I could hear

Bella giggling a little playful giggle. She was up to something, and that something was no good! I slowly made my way into Joshua's room.

Bella was almost eight years old, and she had been introduced to makeup while watching Alison get ready for her day in front of the mirror. It was comical to watch Bella mimic Alison, tilting and turning her head to the side while looking back at the mirror to see how the makeup was dispersed, trying to catch any imperfections before leaving the bathroom for the day. Well, on this day, when I walked into the room to respond to my son's plea for help, I walked in on Bella as she was hunched over Joshua, putting the finishing touches on a full makeup job on Joshua's face. She must have started some time before while Alison and I were still sleeping, because she had a full face mask on Joshua, from eye liner, to blush, to red lipstick. Joshua was covered with makeup, and he wasn't too happy about it. In fact, he was quite livid for a minute or two. I hollered to Alison and forced her out of bed to come and witness the scene. We all laughed, much like we'd laughed years before when Joshua had pulled a fast one on his sister. She was finally even after all these years. I was proud of Joshua because he actually started to laugh as well. At least we knew he could take a joke.

CHAPTER 20

WASHINGTON, DC TRIP

Paul

I put my key into the ignition of the Ford for what seemed like the millionth time. When I turned the key and the engine rolled over, it started with a cough, unlike what I'd experienced before. The engine fired up, but it was skipping a beat. It sounded like it could be water in the gas line or a spark plug misfiring, and as it idled noisily, I made the decision to push on. The old conversion van had served us well for 88,000 miles, and I was hoping to get another 88,000 out of it. After I perused the dashboard for alarms and saw none, I decided that the problem couldn't be major, and I went along with my plans. The van was packed to the hilt, and the final cargo to load that night was Joshua and Isabella. It was a spur-of-the-moment road trip thrown together in two weeks after family friends asked us what we were doing for spring break. With no plans on the calendar, we jumped at the opportunity for adventure. Before we knew it, we were heading to Washington, DC for the trip of a lifetime. Why were we leaving our house at nine p.m. that evening with a remaining stop to make at the Lathion's home to load them and their bags in the van, you might ask? I had driven in DC rush hour traffic before, and I wanted no part of that. I also loved to drive at night when the road was quiet and peaceful. Our ETA for Washington, DC. was after rush hour, so we could just stroll into the mall area and do a little sightseeing before we headed out to our cabin on the Potomac, eleven miles west of the Lincoln Memorial. Everything was planned to the minute for the first twenty-four hours of our trip.

Alison would miss this trip because she needed to get Elsie back to her home in NY. After Alison doled out hugs and kisses and wished us well on our trip, I pulled out of the driveway and stepped on the gas. The engine sputtered in a consistent fashion, so it seemed more and more like a spark plug was skipping a beat. I stepped on the gas while pulling out of the neighborhood onto A1A north, and although the van was a bit sluggish, it got up to speed and rolled along for the next eight miles at fifty MPH with no problems. Gary was standing on the sidewalk as we pulled into his neighborhood. He'd already brought the bags out and lined them up on the sidewalk. Maritza, Tatianna, and Amadeo were making one last trip into the house to grab their remaining travel gear.

I put the van in park and hopped out to help Gary start loading the van. He immediately said, "Bro, what's wrong with the van?"

I shrugged it off and gave him a quick vote of confidence. It had made it the last eight miles with no issues, and we'd take it slow and easy. Gary gave me a look with his big smile and teeth clenched, kind of like he was saying, "I don't know about this." Gary quietly loaded up, and we all packed into the van, ready for the ride of our lives. We said a quick prayer for traveling mercies and rolled out of the neighborhood. The highway was about one and a half miles from their house, and Gary was saying to me "I don't know about this, Paul."

I looked at him and said, "It doesn't seem that bad," as I put my foot to the floor and got a very sluggish and slow response. I didn't want to slow the trip down knowing we couldn't get any issues addressed at ten at night.

The engine was running bad consistently, so I thought it could run consistently bad all night, and we'd pull over in the morning and get it checked out somewhere in Virginia. Gary, not being one to impose his will too often, grinned as if to say, "If you say so," as I continued down the road. About thirty minutes into the trip, I looked over at Gary and asked his opinion again about pushing it through the night. We were about thirty miles south of Brunswick, Georgia, and Gary firmly suggested we pull over in Brunswick, spend the night, and not chance it. I trusted Gary to know that when he made a firm suggestion, it was prudent to take heed.

We skipped along another thirty miles and pulled off I-95 on the second exit for Brunswick. Gary and I decided that rather than unloading the van and moving all of Joshua's equipment into a hotel for the night, we'd pull into a truck stop gas station, keep the engine running for air conditioning and power for Joshua's breathing machine and other equipment, and get five or six hours of sleep, hoping that a mechanic garage would open by seven a.m. It was already after 12:30 a.m. by the time we got situated and settled in. Gary and I were in the front seats of the van. Tati and Isabella were in the rear captain's chairs. Maritza was lying on the floor between the captain's chairs. Amadeo and Josh had the best seats in the house, both sprawled across the bed in the rear of the van. We all laughed a bit and told jokes. Gary and I tried to choose a station with some soul music but we were quickly vetoed. I ended up finding a classical station, and I played it real low as everyone drifted in and out of sleep for the next few hours while parked under blaring lights.

At 6:30 a.m., I decided to start searching on my phone for a place that could check out the van. We were in luck; I happened upon a tire shop that also had a full-service mechanic on staff. I backed the van out. We headed down the road a few miles and pulled into the service shop just before the doors opened for business. The receptionist and mechanic had already clocked in, and they were happy to accommodate us before they started attacking their leftover jobs from the previous day. The mechanic knew what the problem was without even looking under the hood. He did warn us that if the problem was in the front four cylinders, he'd be able to reach it from under the hood, but if not, we'd have to unload the midsection of the van so he could get under the cowling between the two front seats to gain access.

Within thirty seconds of hooking his computer up to the engine, he told us to start unpacking the van. Fortunately, everyone was a little dazed and sleepy and was good-natured about the circumstances, and we were back on our way in about forty-five minutes. This is, of course, after I paid the $345 for a new solenoid, which the mechanic said burn out sporadically in the Ford trucks after about 80,000 miles. He said the next one could go at any time and wished us well. We grabbed a quick fast-food breakfast and started to put miles between us and Jacksonville. We were about nine hours into the trip and eighty miles from where we'd started the night before.

While passing through Savannah later that morning, I had an idea. I'd played with the Baltimore Ravens for my last eleven games in the NFL, and I'd remembered that Matt Stover, our place kicker, was good friends with President George W. Bush's head of secret service. Barack Obama was already in office, and the guard had changed, but I wanted to give it a try anyway. Joshua had complained for days that all he wanted to do for spring break was go to St Augustine, just eighteen miles from our house, rather than travel all the way to boring Washington, DC. I thought that maybe a trip to the White House might change his mind, so I called my friend Matt. Matt answered the phone and said he'd give it a try.

The rest of the trip was uneventful except for the phone call I received from Matt while just an hour south of DC. Matt started asking for social security numbers and told me he thought he could get five of the seven of us in to visit the White House. I felt bad that all of us could not get in, but Maritza and Tati graciously bowed out and told us to go for it. I finished relaying dates of birth and social security information while driving the West Beltway as we headed straight for our cabin on the Potomac River. We arrived at a park which was closed for the season and found our way to a small office where our key had been left. We found our cabin and unloaded the van. It felt good to finally make it to a bed.

It was a brisk day and I felt the cold air against my cheeks as I started to load Joshua's equipment into the van for our trip to the Capitol Building. The cool weather was welcome as Joshua always seemed to breathe more easily when it was not stifling hot with high humidity. Today it was neither. We all piled in and headed east. We found a handicap parking space just a couple of hundred yards from the Capitol. I loaded Joshua into his wagon with his breathing machine, suction machine, and his bag of food with the syringe for feeding and off we went. We were thrilled to see as we drove in that the cherry trees were in full blossom. This was a real treat as they only bloom fourteen days at the most each spring before the flowers fall to the ground. We snapped a few group pictures with us kneeling around Joshua with the tree branches in full bloom behind us. I took a few more pictures of Tati, Bella, and Amadeo climbing the trees amongst the blossoms.

We proceeded to the entrance and were distraught to learn that it was a two-hour wait. I never like to take advantage of our situation, but this time I approached one of the guards and asked for some assistance. Within two minutes, we passed the entire line and were led directly into the rotunda room of the Capitol. The ceiling was 180 feet high, and the walls were covered with paintings depicting important events in our nation's history. We took a few pictures for posterity's sake and proceeded down the hallway to the National Statuary Hall that housed historic marble statues. Each state gave statues of two notable people in their state's history, and thirty-eight of these statues were in this round room. Each statue stood in front of beautiful marble columns that stretched to the ceiling, supporting yet another dome. The building is a true spectacle of architecture. I handed my iPhone to Joshua and Amadeo and turned my back on those two while Gary and I watched Maritza, Isabella and Tati start canvassing the room. Isabella was quite comical while she approached the statues and carried on a conversation with each one. I turned back to Joshua and Amadeo a few minutes later and noticed they were taking pictures of the statues and enjoying the scenery as well. We eventually tired of the room. I walked back to Joshua and asked for my phone back so we could start the tour again. Joshua and Amadeo chuckled a bit, and Joshua pulled my phone away as I reached for it. Thinking something was a little fishy between the two preteen boys, I got more assertive about retrieving my phone. When I got my hands on it and started scrolling through the pictures they'd taken, there was not one picture of Ethan Allen, Samuel Adams, or the great Stephen Austin of Texas, but there was a bunch of high school girls who were obviously on a class trip of some sort. The boys had been clicking shots of girls across the hall! We laughed and proceeded to the next exhibit. All the while, Joshua was still asking why we hadn't just gone to St. Augustine. Typical Josh humor.

The next day was filled with walking the Mall between the Lincoln Memorial and the Washington Monument. We took a stroll with the soldiers cast in iron for the Korean War Veteran Memorial. We walked along the Vietnam Veterans Memorial wall and looked for names of those we knew. We bought a couple of pins from the souvenir trailer, and we read the Gettysburg address on the wall of the Lincoln Memorial. Gary and I stood side by side as we read about some of the historical speeches that had taken place on those steps, arguably the most notable being Martin Luther

King's "I have a dream" speech that literally helped to change a nation. A few steps further east at the edge of the pool, I thought of another speech made by Forest Gump. The sun started going down and we headed to our cabin on the river. It was a good day in DC.

The next morning, the plan was to tour the Arlington Cemetery while making our way to the White House. We were to be at the west gate of the White House at five p.m. sharp, and Agent Pouix would give notice for them to allow five of us through the gate. I had been to Washington, DC for a tour decades before, and I remember Arlington Cemetery left a powerful impression on me, so I anticipated that Joshua and Amadeo would react in much the same way. We parked and unloaded at the welcome house gate, and I proceeded to pull Joshua's wagon with him and all his equipment up and down the steep hills of the cemetery, all the way back to the changing of the guards who honored the Tomb of the Unknown Soldier. We stood in silence and watched from our front row seats. The boys experienced another side of the *Call of Duty* war video games. They were mesmerized.

It was an incredibly beautiful day, and while Isabella was frolicking through the monuments, the sun bounced off her colorful outfit. I thought to myself that it might not have been the best idea to let her dress herself that morning. She had on a tie die shirt that absolutely clashed with her purple sweatpants.

I've heard these seventeen words from Alison many times since reviewing the pictures taken that day. "What was my child wearing that day…? Did you forget you were going to the White House?" As we left the cemetery, while approaching the welcome center, I noticed that any handicapped licensed vehicle could have driven throughout the cemetery, and I quietly shook my head while thinking of my aching back and sore feet. In hindsight, I'm glad I didn't know that was an option, because we really enjoyed the day walking through the monuments and capturing views and angles of the fields and tombs that Joshua would have otherwise missed while riding in the back of the van.

We left Arlington and headed over to the Air Force Memorial and piled out of the van once more. This was a quick visit which knocked out two birds with one stone, because the Pentagon was in full view while standing on the bluff of the Air Force Monument. Joshua and I talked about Chad Hennings, our neighbor from Texas, and how he'd served in the Air Force by flying the A-10 Warthog and flying forty-five missions in Operation Comfort after the first Desert Storm engagement. Chad spoke of dropping supplies in the Turkish mountains to refugees fleeing persecution.

We gave ourselves plenty of time to reach the West Gate of the White House. Had it not been rush hour, I'm sure we would have made it. However, we weren't going to, and I had to call Agent Pouix and apologize. There was no possible way we'd make it to the West Gate, but we were very close to the East Gate. Agent Pouix told me to pull up to the gate and stay put while he called. He asked how many were in the van and said they could stay in the van as we pulled into the gate. The next thing I knew, an arm came out of the guard house window waving me forward. This was absolutely hysterical to us; they were waving a large black conversion van filled with people forward to let us on to the White House grounds. We fully expected to park out on the street! I pulled ahead and stopped at the window. The officer said he was on the phone with Agent Pouix, and that he would give us instructions momentarily. When he hung up the phone, he immediately looked out the window over his left shoulder and pointed about 100 feet away to a maze of concrete barriers placed in a zigzag so that no vehicle could race onto the White House grounds. It reminded me a bit of Lombard Street in San Francisco, the famed "most crooked street in the world." He told me to pull ahead, stop just before the barriers, and put the vehicle in park.

At this point, an officer walking a dog started to approach us, while another officer carried a mirror on a pole that she slid under the van to make sure we were not harboring explosives. After a thorough vetting, she told us to pull ahead slowly and veer right after about fifty yards then head to the massive ornate iron gate and wait. As I slowly inched forward, another officer crept past me, and then a cop on a bicycle rode up alongside, peering into the van to make sure we were friendly. Just as quickly as he'd approached, he peddled away to find another group to investigate. At that moment, we were all alone on the White House grounds, headed toward the most beautiful, massive, ornate iron gates I've ever seen. When we were about twenty feet from the gate, it began to open toward us, both doors swinging out in a slow, majestic manner. I stopped for a moment and quite frankly was a bit dumbfounded that we'd been left alone for a few hundred feet. Little did I know that secret SWAT teams stood atop buildings hidden by shrubs and abutments.

I looked through the gate and just about 100 yards away stood the White House. An agent waved us on and pointed to a row of parking spaces just to the left of the West Wing, just outside of the "Situation Room," where all the world's intelligence agencies report. I think now of the high alert during times of war and terrorist attacks, and how each occurrence that threatened world peace or our safety was digitally streamed through that room to the right of the doors we would enter. Agent Pouix approached the van as I opened the rear door to get Joshua out and situated. He handed each of us pins, hats, and secret service T-shirts, and gave us a great surprise by telling us that all of us were welcome. We hadn't even given them Maritza and Tati's social security numbers and personal information, so they couldn't have done a background check, but I'm sure they did.

There we were, dressed like a bunch of hillbillies, walking through the door of the West Wing while pulling a Red Ryder Wagon that held a boy and his breathing machine. And then, before the tour even started, Isabella asks Agent Pouix if there is a bathroom nearby, she could use. Bella may have been six or seven years old at the time, and as she exited the bathroom, she felt it necessary to holler at the top of her lungs that the bathroom had wooden soap dispensers! We looked like vagabonds and other people were dressed to the nines. We were definitely fish out of water.

The tour began in the Roosevelt room, which was the first cabinet room. We then proceeded to the doorway of the Oval Office, and we all pressed against the Stanchions holding the retention ropes. I must admit it was pretty cool standing in person at the door of the Oval Office. Josh even got a kick out of it in a reverent sort of way.

We proceeded along the West Colonnade, which borders the Rose Garden, and Agent Pouix dutifully gave us the tour guide special, pointing out where the First Lady's Christmas tree was placed every year. We ended up in the Press Briefing Room, that famous blue room that seemed to have nothing in it but a podium with the stamp and seal of the United States of

America on the front. It seemed surprisingly small compared to television. We all stood in front of the podium and struck a pose for the camera. I leaned down and whispered to Josh, "This is a little better than just going to St. Augustine, isn't it?" This time he didn't answer. Well, it was just about over, and as we approached the lobby leading to the exit of the West Wing, Agent Pouix leaned over to me and said that they had a special arrangement waiting for the boys outside in the parking lot.

We exited the West Wing, and they had staged components of all four parts of their defense teams on the grounds. There was a police car with the lights going, an officer on a bike, police dogs, and the biggest thrill for the boys was the SWAT and tactical team all dressed in black with bulletproof garb. To top it off, they carried P90 assault weapons. Amadeo and Josh immediately went wild over the rifles. The SWAT specialist immediately said, "I bet you guys play Call of Duty...We play Call of Duty too, right over there," as he pointed across the parking lot to a window of a room where the guys had their R&R downtime lounge stacked with every Call of Duty and video war game known to man. They gave us a show with the dogs and the assault teams.

As things were winding down, Isabella, noticing shrubs on top of the buildings, blurted out, "Do you guys hide behind those bushes on the roof?" The guy just looked at Isabella and smiled and said, "Now what makes you think that?" He knew he was dealing with a smart six-year-old.

The tour was over and Agent Pouix walked us back to the van. I piled Joshua into the van, and I leaned over him and gave it one last shot. "This is definitely better than just walking down George Street in St. Augustine, right?"

I finally got an emphatic, "YES." And it was only Wednesday.

It was dark and after nine p.m. We hadn't really ventured over to the Washington Monument, so we pulled through the concrete barricades and exited through the west gate, the one we were actually supposed to use earlier that day. We headed one block south and took a left along the edge of the Mall. I pulled over to the right and parked, and the kids, Gary, and Maritza piled out of the van. Bella, Amadeo, and Tati ran to the Washington Monument while Gary and Maritza took a leisurely stroll. Josh was so wiped out that he wanted to pass on the experience and wait in the van. I waited with him until Gary ventured back to the van and goaded me to join Maritza and the kids at the base of the monument. So I did. I got pictures of the kids leaning against the monument looking straight up, all the way to the top. It was a surreal moment that gave me great pleasure, watching our kids enjoy an evening in our country's capital, seeing and doing things that many never get to experience. It was a super end to a very cool day. This was going to be hard to beat for the rest of the trip.

The last hurrah was a trip to the Air and Space Museum, one that the boys treasured and the girls endured. It was a perfect ending to an almost perfect trip, barring engine repairs six days earlier. The ride back was uneventful and except for fueling stops, and a couple food and coffee breaks, we made it back to Jacksonville in under fourteen hours. We made some great memories on that trip.

CHAPTER 21

THE BOY IN THE MIRROR

Joshua continued to defy the odds. He amazed all who knew him with his miraculous recoveries and moments of profound, thought-provoking statements. Sometimes, we as parents gloat about our children with biased and exaggerated conjectures. In Joshua's case, Alison and I could not bestow upon him words to describe the powerful impact he had on every individual who had the opportunity to see inside his heart.

Sometimes we see things more objectively from someone else's perspective.

Mary DeSanto, Joshua's 3rd Grade Teacher

I had the pleasure of having Joshua in my third-grade classroom. As he wheeled into the classroom with his nurse, all I can remember thinking is what a hard life he must be having. He had to lie flat to do his work on a mat because he didn't have the muscle tone to sit up. He was fed through a tube and had to have a full-time nurse with him at all times in case of emergency and for day-to-day needs.

After about ten minutes with Joshua, I realized he did not need my pity or heartache. Joshua was full of life and lived it to the fullest. He loved everything we did in class and everything he did elsewhere. I never saw a single thought of self-pity, but rather a joy to just be on this earth. He could make others laugh so easily just by being himself. There were many times where the class would just sit and laugh at something he said. His smile would light up the classroom more than any other student I have taught. He was truly an inspiration to others with his gentle, humorous ways.

He truly is an angel sent to earth to touch so many lives, mine being one of them.

Josh Heikens, 6th Grade Math Instructor

I had Josh three years ago. At first, I unfortunately didn't know what to expect. I was told that I had to travel to a different classroom each day because there was a boy that had to stay in that room for all his classes.

The school year soon started, and I had a chance to meet Josh. He was always so happy to be at school and, from what I remember, I don't think he missed more than a day of school. He seemed to enjoy his homework, especially a good challenge problem. Even though the homework took him longer to do, he wanted to do every problem just like the rest of the class. It was because of this effort that he carried the highest average in the class as well as the highest average in any of my Pre-Algebra classes.

One of the things I remember from his class was after every test, the kids wanted to know the high score. My response was usually somewhere in the high 90s or even the low 100s. I usually put a bonus problem on the test so sometimes the scores were over a 100 percent. Then, they would ask who received that score. I think I responded all but one time, "Josh Frase." That always put a big smile on his face.

Stacy Norman, 6th Grade Instructor

I had the pleasure of teaching Josh during his sixth-grade year. His classroom connected to mine with a small office that his nurse utilized for medical procedures.

Josh was in my second period for Advanced Reading, but due to his location, I was also able to visit with him between classes. On one of these occasions, I stopped in to talk to him and being my usual clumsy self, I managed to bump into a bottle of his food solution. It didn't just spill, it was more like an explosion of sticky liquid all over me, the classroom and more importantly, Josh. Of course, I panicked and tried to clean it up with anything in arms reach. As I cleaned, the mess just spread, and I was mortified. Suddenly, Josh started laughing at me. I guess I did look funny running around with food dripping out of my hair and into my purse. In his labored and quiet voice, he said, "Don't sweat the small stuff…I'm the one that will be going hungry!" After a moment, we both began to laugh hysterically.

It was then that I realized…I would learn more from Josh than he would ever learn from me.

Sarah McCauslin, 8th Grade Classmate

I met Josh at Landrum Middle School. I remember him being in my history class. He was in my math, too. When I first saw him, my heart sank. I felt so bad. He looked like he couldn't do much until you actually spoke with him, and then you realized how amazing he was. Once I started working with him and talking to him, I learned he was such a sweet person. He had so much heart in him. He didn't let anything hold him back. Nurse Linda and I would always joke around and talk about his video games. He'd whisper, "Hey, how are you?"

His grandma sent me a Bible from New York. When Alison and Paul started verbalizing about his foundation to raise money to help research, I was glad. No one knew how amazing this person was. I didn't see him as having a disability; I saw him as a person who was smarter than I was. He really prompted me to work that much harder. He made me want to do better. People were mean sometimes, but I sat by him every day in history. I said, "I want to work with Josh— I want a good grade!"

Sarah McCauslin's Letter to Joshua

Josh,
When I started writing you this, I wasn't sure what to say. Not that I couldn't think of anything but that there probably wouldn't be enough room. I have heard nothing but good things and praise about you. How much of a joy to have you in teacher's classes, how outstanding you are and all around

amazing as well. I treasured the experience of having you in my world and in my class last year. Mainly, I wanted to say how strongly I admire you. You exceed teacher's expectations and strive to do your best in everything you do. I was always the one wanting to be your partner because you taught me, made me learn more. Your parents are also an inspiration. If there was one good thing they did in their lives, it was to bring you into the world. You give me a sense of hope and strength, to push myself to be better and to try my best. I want to be a better person because of you. I am very grateful to have the privilege to attend PVHS with you. Words can't express how much you mean to so many people. From your birth in 1995, you have brought so many smiles to people's faces. You shine such a bright light on so many people.

Max Ervanian, 9th Grade Classmate

Josh was a great guy to be around with. He always made you laugh, and he always worried about everyone else before himself, even on days when he wasn't feeling that great.

Later along in that year, the National Honor Society renamed their chapter to the Josh Frase Chapter in honor and dedication to Josh Frase with all the lives he has touched and influenced not just at the school or in the community, but on a state and national level!

Karen Maguire, 9th Grade Algebra 1 Teacher, Ponte Vedra High School

Before school started, the principal called a meeting of all Joshua's teachers. He said, "We have a student who has special needs. He will be wheeled in on a bed. He'll need oxygen. He'll tire easily." He wanted to prepare us so that we could overcome any obstacles and so that we could prepare to teach Joshua properly. I had a hard time with this at first, worrying about how effective I would be in the classroom in teaching him. I thought, *how am I going to handle this challenge?*

I wrote a letter to Paul at the end of the year telling him I put Josh up there as probably one of the greatest teachers I've ever had. Our roles had reversed. He taught me. He taught me about perseverance, attitude, and persistence. The smile on his face—his sense of humor thrown in with all of this that he had to battle; the one-line zingers…we all just would crack up. I can remember handing out a big packet of something to study for the end of course exam. We tried to condense the work to save paper. He said, "She's got to be kidding."

I told him, "You don't need to do the whole packet—you have the highest average in the class." He knew what he was doing— he didn't need it. He'd do it anyway. I'd say, "You didn't have to do it."

He'd roll his eyes and say, "I did it because I knew I could, and…he'd look at Nurse Linda, "besides, she makes me."

He had the highest average in the school for Algebra One. It was amazing how well he understood. He could have been in honors, but he said, "No thanks— I'm trying to balance my life." He was very quick— picking up new concepts— received an Award of Excellence for Algebra One. What an honor it's been to teach JOSH!

He had this light about him— I can't even describe how he would make me feel.

We named our National Honor Society Chapter after him. The Joshua Frase Chapter of the National Honor Society of Ponte Vedra High School. Josh embodied all the qualities, but he did not want to be the center of attention.

Nkumu's Mandungu, Family, Tribute to Joshua Miles Frase

When reflecting on the most defining moments of my life, the wonderful visits I have had with Joshua Miles Frase certainly figure amongst those moments. Joshua's wisdom, gentle heart, strength, unselfishness, and amazing sense of humor reflect God's amazing personality and are a great source of inspiration and strength.

The wonderful moments during which me and the "Big Fellow" as I affectionately came to call him, discussed a myriad of topics ranging from history and politics to science and pop culture, expanded my outlook on life and energized me. The nature of our conversations would almost always entail an earnest attempt to solve issues, answer the why's of history both past and present, and discuss a variety of how's e.g., why Sparta's warrior culture never survived, how some of the armed conflicts currently raging throughout the world came to prevail, and some potential immediate solutions, such as Balkanization, Instituting federation-like autonomy, etc.

We'd also discuss how the latest advances in regenerative medicine granted our wounded veterans a better quality of life; the imminent changes in the field of regenerative science; the seemingly boundless potential of the field, etc.

Early on, Joshua's remarkable intellect was undeniable. His ability to simplify and generate practical solutions to relatively complex issues was apparent. He consistently displayed the knowledge, analytical skills, and wisdom of someone well beyond his years. These amazing attributes quickly led me to realize, as I often shared with Grandma Elsie, that Joshua's gift was his mind. His mind, which he diligently exercised and stimulated, is one of the sharpest I have ever encountered. More importantly, his gentle and kind nature, which was a testament to Uncle Paul and Aunt Alison's overwhelming kindness, love, and generosity, made him a delight to speak to and interact with.

Concerning Joshua's strength, I can think of very few human beings who consistently displayed this attribute in the face of ongoing adversity, to the extent that Joshua did. Day in and day out he let his light shine and did not allow his condition to define him. When I'd visit with Joshua and witness his daily routine, which was relatively labor intensive, I could not help but admire the fact that he did not complain. Instead, he'd focus on the positive aspects of life, such as the latest in gaming technology, school science projects, and endeavors that he and his friends had recently undertaken. In these conversations and interactions, Joshua's unselfishness consistently stood out.

Despite having a wealth of knowledge and being undoubtedly smart, Joshua did not seek to be the center of attention. He'd often spend a lot of time asking me what I thought regarding the many topics that we'd discuss, and he displayed a genuine interest in hearing and understanding my opinions. He reflected a great deal of maturity. Most amazingly, I have since firmly identified that this ability to attentively focus on others and get others engaged, which Joshua displayed, is a key characteristic of great leaders. The ability to make a conversation not about himself but rather about the person with whom he is interacting and thereby making that person feel valuable, whether intended or not, added to Joshua's uniqueness and again displayed maturity well beyond his years. In similar fashion, his sense of humor, which reminded me of Grandpa, also set him apart.

Gary Lathion, Family Friend

Wow, where do I start? So many wonderful memories with Josh and the Frase family that I might not get it all in on the first email.

Let me start by saying that I have been truly blessed, impacted, inspired, touched, changed, compelled, motivated, loved, challenged, undone, and more to have met Joshua Miles Frase. To reflect on the special times that I was honored to share with him, there are a few times that really stand out. Most would not know or understand the tenacious spirit that Josh had when it came time to be rewarded for good grades or behavior. You see, looking past the exterior, most couldn't guess he was an honor student, or the fact that he loved PlayStation games. He always knew about the latest games and didn't hesitate to ask about getting them. My son, Amadeo, and Josh spent many hours playing these games together. You see, on the inside Josh was a normal teenager when it came to things like that. He just didn't want the fun to stop. Many times Amadeo spent the night on the weekend to continue the party. You nearly had to have a power outage to get them to stop playing. They really had a good time together. This led to trips like Ichetucknee Springs where we inner tubed down the river, camping at Little Talbot Island, and the Washington, DC trip.

A time that has a special place in my heart is the time that we went to spend some away time in Ararat, Virginia, up in the mountains in a home that was at least 100 years old that had been completely restored. One of the most attractive points at this location was that there was no cable and very poor cell phone reception. Yeah, we got to really talk to one another.

Well one morning it was kinda wet outside and it seemed best for Josh to stay indoors while everyone else went on a nature hike. To keep Josh company, we didn't have a TV to turn on or video games but, in the house, there was a set of books about the Civil War. These weren't your average books either. They had rare pictures of the soldiers, battlefields, weapons used, etc. I selected the book related to the battles. I thought Josh would enjoy it if I read to him. I started reading, and he was so quiet I thought his mind was somewhere else or maybe I was making him sleepy. So, to test my theory, I asked Josh a few questions regarding the battle and to my amazement, not only did he recall what I read, but we also discussed the mistakes this general had made. This went on for hours till it was past ten o'clock at night. It was great because I was getting into it too. I'll never forget special times like these.

Letter from Amadeo Lathion, Best Friend

Dear Josh,

I don't even know where to start...u have filled my life with so much adventure from the little model airplanes we used to build—to entering the Whitehouse and seeing the historical wonders it beholds. Josh, for one thing your presence here on earth has taught me so much...the day I met you on the beach being any average young boy, I approached you with kindness and curiosity. I honestly had never talked to anyone who was disabled before simply because I wasn't sure if they were like me... laughing...playing...a friend.

Then as I began to talk more, I realized people like Josh are exactly like me...The absolutely only thing Josh couldn't do is get up and walk around. I remember coming over to Josh's house right when I first met him. We always wanted to build a model; it basically became a routine for a while. I couldn't leave until Josh and I had built something. Then some years had passed and now we began checking out the remote-control stuff: airplanes, flight simulators, models, slot cars, rockets! It wasn't too long till we visited the local hobby store and walked in and were overwhelmed by all the different things it had. Josh was pointing at all different directions. I would get whatever he was pointing at and bring it down and show it too him…Then he pointed to her…She was the most beautiful thing Josh and I had ever seen…BIG BERTHA…I brought her down and me and Josh quickly flipped the package over to see how high and fast she could go. Josh and I had reached the ROCKET ERA!

We brought it home and over time began working on it carelessly spraying highlighter orange spray paint on the rocket which at the time we didn't realize, not so smart…Well, although Josh's bed sheets were covered in orange spray marks, we finally had completed the rocket. Mr. Tom was with Josh one day when I came over so we had asked if he could take us out to the nearest soccer field to shoot it off. I gave Josh the remote with the button to push so it could launch…

Josh pushed the button and BIG BERTHA was OFF! I looked up in the air, and I looked back at Josh. There was a great deal of excitement in his eyes. This was one of many things Josh and I did.

Then the Video Game ERA came along and next thing you know models started to collect dust, and topics changed from the biggest model in the hobby store to the next CALL OF DUTY…And unfortunately, that's where Josh and I found ourselves stuck in as I speak, THE VIDEO GAME ERA.

But what have I been given from all of this? Josh has Myotubular Myopathy…As I walk with Josh simply going to the store and looking around, I see one man take a stare at Josh. I began to wonder why? Josh is like you and I. Most people wouldn't take the time to come up or say, "Hi," when they see someone of Josh's manner…In fact, it's a treasure or honor to meet someone disabled because they truly change your life. You come to realize just how grateful you are to be able to get out of bed in the morning or to clean and do morning chores. Anytime I don't want to do something or feel too lazy to get up and do it, Joshua Frase is the one motivation that makes me get up. He makes you so grateful for a strong heart or the ability to breathe on your own. He has given me appreciation for what I have. And although receiving a material gift is nice, receiving a gift that cannot be seen is a million times better, because you cannot take that material gift to heaven or have it your whole life. So the next time you see a person or meet someone that is physically or mentally disabled, don't be afraid to say hi or wave even if they cannot see or understand you, because I have gained so much from just waving and approaching this young man one day on the beach. Thank You, Josh, for everything and especially a friendship that will never be forgotten.

This is the boy in the mirror.

CHAPTER 22

REAL COURAGE

Paul

People have commented that it took a lot of courage to play football in the National Football League. While I can't shape the definition of one's idea of courage, I would say it took little courage, little bravery, a lot of passion for the game, and a loose screw. I woke up on Sunday mornings during the fall with a passion for football, a passion for the contest, a passion to win, just like every other guy in the league. The passion was building and grew as we approached the coin toss in anticipation of the controlled chaos that was about to commence. I'm sure you've seen it on TV every game day; the camera focused on guys jumping up and down in the tunnel, getting psyched up. There's nothing that compares to the feeling of looking through the facemask in a bridled frenzy, a barely contained desire to crash, hit, dominate, and win.

The captains of each team meet the referees at the fifty-yard line. The coin is tossed; heads or tails, and one team celebrates receiving the ball, while the other team conjures up a lot of bravado and says, "Yes, now our defense can show them what we got, let's shut 'em down," while at the same time, wishing they'd won the coin toss. Every possession of the ball is vital. The whistle blows and I find myself standing in the wedge, watching the kicker approach the tee to drive his foot through the pigskin. Watching the ball sail over my head, I look back to the oncoming train to pick my man out of ten frothing at the mouth lunatics. I look back over my shoulder to see my kickoff return specialist catch the ball, and then start on my quest to take on the 250-pound wedge buster, who happened to be running full speed. My weapon of choice is my cranium, my frontal lobe encased in a plastic shell with a quarter inch steel cage surrounding my face, protecting my pearly whites. I clearly recall one of my front teeth exploding on impact while ear-holing Thurman Thomas, a common and effective tactic of that day, during one of the contests with the Bills. Sometimes that steel cage of protection has a hard time doing its job.

Courage on the football field is what it took to get back up off the ground after a sixty-minute contest of the opponent getting the better of you. It didn't happen often for this eleven-year veteran, but it did happen. I distinctly remember one afternoon playing the LA Rams in Anaheim, California, and consistently brushing myself off seven out of ten times that day as Jackie Slater, a perennial pro-bowler who ended up playing eighteen years in the league, took me to school, play after play after play.

Real courage was not taught on the gridiron. Back then, my definition of courage was one-dimensional. It focused on our armed forces and what the brave men and women in our military sacrifice. But that all changed when my son was born. A new dimension of courage was impressed on my psyche the second I witnessed my son gasping for his first breath, writhing in frustration because he could not draw in the air he needed to breathe. His skin color grew blotchy with shades of red, white, and purple, all mixed together due to the lack of oxygen. My lesson in courage was just beginning, and my teacher was an infant.

In June of 2010, while addressing a TEDx audience, Brene Brown, a research professor at the University of Houston, defined courage. She explained that the root of the word courage comes from the Latin word "cor," meaning heart, and the early definition of the word when it was introduced to the English language was, "to tell the story of who you are with your whole heart." *Talk Like Ted*, Carmine Gallo (New York: St. Martin's Press, 2014), 51. What Alison and I witnessed over the next 5,800 days of his life, was a baby, a young boy, and then a young man, tell the world who he was with his *whole heart*.

It started for me the first time I saw Joshua crying, when I saw his red face scrunched together and his mouth agape, crying as well as he could. The muscles in his chest and his diaphragm were too weak to expel air fast enough past the vocal cords to cause vibration and make a sound. He was telling me who he was without a sound. A few days after Joshua was born, the doctors had pronounced Joshua blind and deaf. I sat with my face six inches from my son's, and I moved very slowly, watching Joshua's eyes track me. He was not blind, and he was telling me who he was with his whole heart. Days later, when we determined he was not deaf through witnessing Joshua move his right hand to the beat of the boom box we had playing at the top of his hospital bed, I knew Alison and I could tell him who we were with our whole hearts, but more importantly, we could tell him who he was and what he meant to us. And he could hear us.

The following days, months, and years, we witnessed Joshua continuously exclaiming who he was with his whole heart. He fought to smile, to giggle, and to laugh. He fought to breathe, to talk, and to stand in a standing frame. He fought to get well, and to get out of the hospital numerous times. He fought day in and day out to survive, to live, and to thrive. Joshua told us countless times through his will and his fight, who he was with his whole heart; he revealed to Alison and me the true definition of courage. We never once in those 5,800 days heard Joshua complain about his disorder, about being trapped in that body. I witnessed his courage every time a young person would stare at him, some in wonderment and some in horror. When I felt like putting my hands around their scrawny little necks and squeezing just a little, I witnessed Joshua shrug off their ignorance…they didn't know, How could they if their parents hadn't brought them to an understanding? Some of the parents were worse than the children. We witnessed his courage when he'd invite friends over to play Play-Station™; he'd usually kick their tail. He did this while lying in bed or on the floor in the living room. I witnessed his courage while in high school, being pushed on a gurney down the halls to his next class. It was in high school where I witnessed most of the kids demonstrating their courage by not staring and by waving and saying, "Hey Josh," Josh would always give a wave back. We witnessed his courage when he was honored at the National Honor Society induction at the Ponte Vedra High School. The teachers made sure Joshua was front and center, his gurney and all, to accept his awards. Ultimately, Alison and I witnessed Joshua's courage in his desire to be the first boy through clinical trials, to risk his life and to test an unproven therapy for the very first time for his peers. He told us who he was with his whole heart through his courage.

I had a conversation with Jim Kelly (famous quarterback of the Buffalo Bills in the 80s and 90s) about our battle scars, physical and emotional. At the time of our conversation, Jim had recently undergone major spine surgery placing plates and screws in his lower back to hold him together. I had experienced back surgery while still playing. I stepped on the field forty days after surgery to play the Carolina Panthers while with Green Bay. The bottom of my left foot is still numb almost two decades later. Jim discussed his feat of making it to the Super Bowl four years in a row (which will probably never be matched), and then lamented a bit about never winning one of those contests. I mentioned my despair of finally making it to the Super Bowl in my 10th season but then losing the world championship game.

The conversation got a little more sobering when Jim mentioned he'd lost three of his offensive linemen already, to different maladies...All were under fifty years of age. I knew each of them as I'd played against them as many as fourteen times. We spoke of how the average life span of an NFL lineman who plays more than three years in the league is an abysmal fifty-three years old...a statistic that I would like to avoid by three or four decades.

Then our conversation turned to our boys. Jim and his wife Jill lost their only son at the age of eight to a terrible disorder called Crabbe's disease. Jim and I had swapped responsibilities showing up for each other's fundraisers to raise money for our respective foundations. Jim knew that Joshua was a fighter just like his son, Hunter. The courage our sons showed us was immeasurable, and we've been blessed beyond capacity.

So, it takes courage to play in the NFL? Eh, maybe a smidgen...but real courage is revealed through how we respond to adversity. How we respond sends a resounding message of who we are with our whole heart. Thank you, Joshua, for teaching us this crucial lesson.

CHAPTER 23

DECEMBER TWENTY-FOURTH

Paul

It was 12:47 a.m. on Christmas Eve, 2010. Joshua and I were up later than normal due to the start of his Christmas break, sitting in front of the television. We were watching some awful recently produced Baby New Year show, and Christmas was still twenty-four hours away. Joshua was lying in bed, and I was sitting in my office chair between his bed and the cabinet that held his TV, Play-Station 2™, and all of his models, CDs, and games.

I told Joshua that the show was nauseating, and that we needed to watch something else, and he wholeheartedly agreed. I looked down at his DVDs and saw one that had been sitting in the same place for over a month. Our friend Gary had raved about this DVD for well over a month and said that it affected his whole family in a powerful way. Feeling a little guilty that we had not watched it to this point, I mentioned to Joshua that it was time to put it in the player and watch it, so we did.

Chris Tomlin, a contemporary Christian artist, and Louie Giglio, a prominent youth preacher from Atlanta, were on tour when this DVD was produced. It was called the *Indescribable Tour*, and Louie would be Chris Tomlin's intermission act in between sets. Josh and I watched intently, as the next forty-two minutes of digital recording changed both of our lives.

Louie Giglio's message was essentially a word that our God, the Creator of all things, and the master of the universe, was enormous, and we were small, but we were not insignificant in His plan. He demonstrated this by showcasing the stars and the planets, and the whole *known universe*. He showed how our galaxy was 100,000 light years from edge to edge, and that one light year—how far light travels in one year at 299,792 kilometers per second—was 5.88 trillion miles. He followed that by saying, "You try to do the math." He then said that our galaxy is just one of billions of galaxies out there. Louie then started showing pictures of galaxies taken by the Hubble Telescope. He said that God's so immense, and he was probably up there laughing, saying "Go build a bigger telescope and bring it up here, and I'll blow your mind." During the last seven minutes of Louie's talk, he winds it down by showing just one more galaxy that is thirty-one million light years away called the Whirlpool galaxy, and he shows a particular cluster of stars that looked like a white cotton ball. It is called the X-Structure, and it's in the middle of the Whirlpool Galaxy. In the center of this cluster of stars is a black hole the shape of an X, and tilted just a bit on its side, the black hole resembles a cross. He quickly states that he's not a scientist, and he's not going to say that God put a black hole the shape of a cross in the middle of the Whirlpool galaxy. His point was that if one takes the time to contemplate the universe, there's no denying that the God who created the universe has his thumb prints all over his creation for us to observe and enjoy.

I have to admit I was dozing off a bit during the last five minutes of the recording, but I caught the message clearly, and as the credits were rolling, and Chris Tomlin's song "Indescribable" was playing, I looked over my left shoulder at Joshua and looked into his eyes in amazement. Joshua's eyes were as wide as saucers, and they sparkled with wonderment and astonishment. Joshua said to me while he was staring at the stars in the background of the rolling credits, "Dad, did you see what God did? Did you see what God did?"

I replied, "Yes, Josh, isn't it amazing how big and how great our God is?" I leaned across his bed and ran my fingers through his hair as I kissed his cheek. Yes Josh, I saw what God has done, and it's nothing short of amazing. It was 1:50 a.m. and it was time to shut the lights off.

We awoke about 8:30 a.m., and I proceeded to go through my morning routine with Joshua. I would unhook him from the monitors and give him his morning bath. I then gave him his morning nebulizer and cough-assist routine, cleaning out his airways and lungs to get him ready for his day.

Around 10:30, Alison came home after spending the morning with her mother, who was ailing with Parkinson's, at the nearby hotel. This was the morning of Christmas Eve, and both Alison and I were in a hurry to get the day started, as we had a lot to do before tomorrow's celebration of Christ's birthday. We were just like most parents of the Judeo-Christian faith on this morning across the country, a little frantic and planning as efficient a day as possible.

I had to run to the hardware store two miles north on A1A and I would be back in just fifteen minutes or so. While I was there, I ran into Tom Dempsy, a friend who had sold me both of my Harley Davidson motorcycles years before. I hadn't seen Tom in at least ten years, so I spent an extra fifteen minutes catching up. Thirty minutes later, about 11:15 a.m., I walked in the door. I went straight to Joshua's room to give him a shot of his morning food through his G-tube. As I walked around his bed and picked up the syringe to fill it with food, to my horror, I noticed Joshua was not breathing. The BiPap was not running. I yelled out, "Alison, he's not breathing! Get in here now!"

Alison burst into the room and started giving directions; she grabbed the Ambu bag from me and told me to make sure there was plenty of oxygen pumping from the 100-pound liquid oxygen tank that was in Joshua's closet. Alison told Isabella to run across the street and tell our neighbor, Dr. Escobar, to come quickly, and that Joshua had stopped breathing. She told me to call 911 so I ran into the kitchen to grab the house phone and called 911. As I was talking to the 911 operator, Alison was giving the dismal picture for me to relay…that he was non-responsive, that his color was still ashen gray, and that we were checking for a pulse. At that moment, Dr. Escobar ran into the room with Isabella right behind. Dr. Escobar went directly to Alison's side, made an assessment, and began to pump Joshua's chest to see if he could aid the heart to re-engage. I picked Isabella up and carried her out of Joshua's room, as this was not a good scene for Bella to experience.

I stayed with Bella for a couple of minutes, until one of the neighbors came in the door, and I handed her off to them. I ran back into Joshua's room and saw Dr. Escobar pumping Joshua's chest while Alison held the Ambu bag and oxygen for Dr. Escobar to administer while he was working on Joshua. Alison and I were both speaking to Josh, "Stay with us Josh, BREATHE, you can do it Josh…"

We had been through this before, and we were able to revive him. This time was going to be no different than the dozens of times before. We would end up in the hospital for a few days and come home. We'd celebrate Christmas at the hospital, a new experience, but we'd make the best of it and bring Christmas to Joshua in the hospital if need be. Dr. Escobar and Alison worked non-stop on Joshua until the EMTs arrived. I had moved Alison's car out of the garage because I knew they would bring the gurney into the house through the garage, as it was the straightest shot to Joshua's room. I sprinted back outside to brief and guide the EMTs to Joshua's room. They rushed to Joshua's side as Dr. Escobar gave one of them the report. They knew we were fighting the clock, so they moved Joshua onto the gurney as quickly as possible, cleared everything, and wheeled Joshua out of his room, across the kitchen, and out the door into the garage. They rushed down the driveway with Alison by their sides still administering breaths with the Ambu bag.

An adrenaline rush that I'd experienced many times before was in full force. Alison was giving directives, and everyone was jumping and doing. I came up to the side door of the ambulance and peered in, witnessing Alison draped over Joshua, giving him breaths, and talking softly to him. I looked into my son's glassy eyes and knew that this was not the Joshua we'd revived what seemed like a hundred times before; he was still non-responsive.

Alison and I were still determined to do everything in our power and begged God to touch Joshua one more time. As I was leaning into the ambulance, I began to feel anger well up from deep within my soul, and I took my left hand, which had been resting against the side of the door, raised it up as I formed a fist, and I punched the side of the ambulance.

It was time to close the doors, and as I watched the ambulance pull away with its siren blaring, I prayed like I had never prayed before. I also felt an anger that I'd never felt before. I turned and walked up the driveway, weaving in and out of our neighbors, about fifteen in all, who had congregated to give us support. I reached the garage in a rage, and I was looking for something to pummel. There was an empty three-foot by three-foot wreath box sitting next to the garbage cans, and I screamed at the top of my lungs, "SON OF A BITCH," as I kicked the box as hard as I could. I walked into the house and fell into the zone. I carried out my normal routine of gathering Joshua's equipment he would need and started loading it into the van. I was going to the hospital to give them what they needed to care for Joshua, my son, my only son...who was non-responsive.

I threw the remaining items I needed in a gym bag and ran out the door to the van. I just knew that by now Alison had been successful in reviving Joshua and he was on his way to recovery. Our neighbor, Cliff, from across the street calmly walked up to me and asked if he could drive me, and I shrugged off his request, feeling like I could do it. Cliff gently but firmly said he wanted to drive, so I handed him the keys and ran around the van to the passenger door. The second I put my hand on the door handle to open the door, it felt like a strong electrical charge entered my body and ripped through my hand, then throughout the rest of my body, landing in and on my chest. Cliff started the car and rolled down the driveway into the street. He calmly asked what hospital they had taken Joshua to, and I said, "Beaches Baptist," which was quite unusual, because normally we would have gone to Wolfson Children's Hospital for the best care around. But this time, because Joshua never responded at home, they wanted to get him stabilized as quickly as possible. The Beaches hospital was only fifteen minutes away versus a forty-five-minute drive to Wolfson. About 500 yards from our driveway, we took a left turn and headed north on A1A. Beaches Baptist was about 6.5 miles north in Jacksonville Beach.

As we headed north, I had my teeth clenched and found myself breathing rhythmically: inhale, and slowly exhale, inhale and slower exhale. The anger I'd felt before was giving way to numbness, an *in the zone* type of feeling. Within two miles from our house, I found myself gently rocking back and forth to the rhythm of my breathing. My throat began to tighten, and my breathing velocity increased, like it was being tuned to a metronome, and the metronome was moving in short and concise counts, instead of a four count, it rose to an eight count and a sixteen count. I quickly realized I was in this mode to stop myself from completely falling apart. In just another mile, I understood why Cliff had been insistent on driving, as I had all I could do to keep it together, rocking and breathing. The 6.5 miles seemed to drag on forever, and as Cliff was weaving in and out of traffic and maneuvering through the obstacle course that separated me from my son and my wife, I was experiencing a surreal and poignant moment. I was focused on the fact that my son had been non-responsive when I last saw him, but I was confident that when I arrived at the hospital, I would find Joshua intubated and breathing, his color coming back from gray to pink, his eyes not glassed over but closed while he was resting peacefully after the trauma he'd experienced thirty minutes prior.

As soon as Cliff pulled up in front of the emergency room, I snapped out of the dream state. I hopped out of the van and ran in to assess the situation to find out what equipment I needed to bring in. I was running down the hall and saw a flurry of people at the end room. The emergency exit door was just to the left of the room they had Joshua in. I ran straight to Alison. She was frantically saying to pray and telling me that they were still working on Joshua, trying to get him to respond. She brought me into the vacant patient room to the left of the emergency exit. There were four or five people in the room circled together holding hands, praying for Joshua. One of the nurses was in the room praying as well. Alison and I were begging God to give Joshua the strength to breathe. Alison looked up at that moment and saw Dr. Schaeffer, Joshua's pulmonologist, walking toward us. Alison greeted him and gave him an assessment, and Dr. Schaeffer joined the team of doctors in Joshua's room for a few minutes.

This was the first time in almost sixteen years in a hospital setting that we were not given access to Joshua. Normally, Alison would have been right at Joshua's side speaking to Joshua and consulting with the doctors about his care. This was a necessity, especially if there was a new doctor present that had never dealt with Joshua before and who needed to be guided in Joshua's care. This was not the case today. There were all new faces, a new resident in training, and this time there was nothing that Alison could assist with. There was nothing we could do but wait and pray. Joshua was still non-responsive.

I calculated that the doctors worked on Joshua another twenty minutes or so. Friends began trickling into the ER and stood with us in the vacant room and outside Joshua's door. Alison and I would get to the opening of Joshua's room and peer in to see if there was any progress, and when we heard that none had been made, we would fall back into the hallway and pray a bit while calling other friends and family to tell them to start a prayer chain for Joshua. The commotion in Joshua's room began to subside, and slowly, one by one, a nurse, a PA, a doctor would sift out of the room. Notably, they all avoided us and walked to the nurses' station. Finally, a doctor emerged and gave us the news that Joshua was gone. Doctor Schaeffer walked behind him, crying profusely. Joshua had been his patient for the better part of fifteen years.

Everything from that point fell back into the surreal, and Alison and I were attached to each other. We entered Joshua's room to find him lying on his left side. As I approached Joshua, I reached out for him and draped myself across his body, putting my face in his hair. My tears began to flow down my cheek and onto his hair, and my chest began to heave. I remember wailing, "My son, my son."

Our pastor, who was standing behind Alison and me, gently put his hand on my shoulder and said, "Your son is not here anymore…He's with his heavenly father." Both Alison and I knew this, as this was our belief and our hope. Joshua was in Christ's arms, and Joshua was standing tall and strong.

I remember holding Alison and her saying she needed some fresh air. She was struggling to breathe. We walked out the emergency exit and Alison surrendered her fight. She fell to the pavement and lay faced down as uncontrollable sobs racked through her body. After a bit, Alison got up and we made the calls that needed to be made—one of them to Alan Beggs. Alison asked him if he needed tissue samples from Joshua, and he said, "No, Alison, Joshua has already given so much to research." Then we planned our next step which was to go straight to Elsie's room at the hotel and to have Isabella meet us there to share the news. Isabella had made it to the Fonville's home and was being kept busy with their four kids. Alison called and asked Kathryn to bring Isabella to the hotel. When we felt we had covered our bases, we climbed into our pastor's car as he'd offered to take us to the hotel. He prayed words of peace and comfort over us as we sat in the back seat, talking softly to each other, both of us in disbelief, being forced to face reality, and being forced to bring the news to one of Joshua's fiercest warriors, his Nanna Rockett.

When we arrived at the hotel and walked into the lobby, we were greeted by many of our dear friends. We are blessed to have a handful of couples that embraced us for who and what we were as a family. They embraced us, and they embraced our son with genuine, altruistic motives, and they always included us during the holidays. We hugged a bit, cried a bit, and excused ourselves after a few minutes as Elsie and Isabella awaited our arrival on the fourth floor.

Alison and I entered the elevator, and I pushed the button for the fourth floor. We did not speak a word, but we were in sync for what we had to do. We were about to tell a brave little nine-year-old sister, and a strong seventy-nine-year-old Nanna, that they had just lost a brother and a grandson…her only brother, and her only grandson. The aid opened the door, and as I walked into the room, I saw Nanna sitting in the chair up against the window with a footstool in front of it. I believe Kathryn had already brought Bella to the hotel room, and with the help of Lissa Slade, had gotten Bella up the elevators while avoiding all of the friends waiting for Alison and me in the lobby.

The rest of the day was a blur to me. We spent the next thirty minutes sharing with Nanna and Isabella that Joshua had gone on to heaven. It was absolutely heart wrenching to see Bella wail uncontrollably and to see the tears running down Nanna's cheeks. I remember driving to our house and being greeted at our door by Anthony and Debbie Schmidt, who'd been called an hour earlier by Kevin Acavedo, who shared that Joshua was at the hospital. Anthony and his daughter Christina were out finishing last minute shopping when they got the call. Anthony stopped what he had been doing and went straight for the hospital. When he arrived, he raced back into the ER. He quickly realized that we were gone, and the doctors were gone, and he knew Joshua was too.

Anthony called his wife Debbie, and they, being caring friends and people of action, orchestrated food, and calls to many people, all of which were invited to our home to share in our suffering and to comfort us. It was late afternoon when we arrived home. There were many hugs, tears, and condolences shared. The stories of Joshua were nonstop, and they went on well into the night.

I don't recall when everyone left, but I do recall lying with Alison until she'd fallen asleep. Then I wandered across the living room and into Joshua's room, collapsing on his bed, where I'd been sleeping the last four years. I became Joshua's night nurse at the time the insurance altered our policy. I did not shut the light off, and I remember staring at the ceiling, falling into deep bouts of crying and bewilderment. Our son was no longer with us. I rolled onto my right side and stared at the pillow where Joshua's head had rested for nearly eight years, and then I'd roll on my back and stare at the ceiling again. This went on until the early morning hours before my eyes dried up, and I became weary enough to fall asleep for a short period of time. I awoke to the nightmare still blaring in my mind and the light still on. I rolled to my left to flip the switch. When the light flickered off, I realized that dawn was upon us, and a quiet and subtle glow was peering through the shades. I slowly sat up, looked back over my right shoulder and pictured Joshua in bed beside me, but reality flooded my mind, and the tears began to flow once again.

I got up and walked back across the living room to our master bedroom and quietly crawled in bed with Alison. As I lay down beside Alison, she awoke with a startle, and her chest immediately began to heave as the tears began to flow again. I just held her. We'd lost our firstborn child. How do you face that reality? And on Christmas morning of all days? Ordinarily, we'd always congregate in the living room, Joshua on his mat and Bella buzzing around. We'd read Luke chapter 2 and then the games would begin, but not this Christmas. Alison and I were crying again when we heard little feet scurrying across the living room floor. In popped our beautiful and joyful prize, our Bella. She immediately climbed up on top of the fluffy down comforter and stretched out on top of Alison's chest. She wiped Alison's tears away with her pajama sleeve, and she said, "Mommy, please don't cry. Joshua is having the best Christmas ever because he can see Jesus, but we can't." At that moment, Alison and I felt a release of emotion without the tears. It took our precious nine-year-old Bella to bring clarity back to our house on Christmas morning. Yes, Joshua was having the best Christmas ever, just not with us.

Joshua's earthly journey had come to an end, but his eternity with his Creator had just begun. This, and the fact that he'd met his Grandpa

Rockett face to face for the first time brought solace to Alison and me on this Christmas day of 2010, and it gave us the courage to celebrate Christmas as we had planned with friends and family. He was not here. He was in a better place.

CHAPTER 24

DECEMBER TWENTY-FOURTH
Alison

I brought mom down to Florida after our annual girl's trip to the Big Apple with Isabella. New York is magical at Christmastime, and it was important to me that Isabella experienced the same enchanted world of my childhood. Mom was entering into the advanced stages of Parkinson's. I knew this was perfect timing to bring her home with us for the holidays.

At that point in her disorder, she required daily assistance with her care. In New York, she had a caregiver living with her. Taking her home to Florida for a spell meant that I would become her caretaker. We put her up in a hotel with a handicap bathroom for ease of care and brought her to our home during the day. This allowed me to care for both Joshua and my mom at the same time. Paul spent nights with Joshua, and I spent the night with mom at the hotel.

It was as important for my mom as it was for Joshua that they got to spend a lot of time together. Those two shared a bond unlike any other. Oftentimes I would find her standing by his bed, holding his hand. Occasionally they would talk, but often, they'd just sit in each other's presence, stealing looks at each other. They spent the whole evening of the 23rd like that. I had to peel her away from his bed to take her to the hotel.

The morning of the 24th, I came home from the hotel just as Paul was leaving for errands. He updated me on Joshua's morning: he'd had his breathing treatment; he started his food. Isabella and Joshua were hanging out on his bed, playing per their usual. I immediately began preparing for

Christmas day. I was exhausted from the night before. Mom was up several times throughout the night, and it drained me.

My list was long, and my energy was low. I looked at my list and began crossing things off it. Shortly after eleven, Joshua and Isabella began to argue, and frustrated by the distraction, I sent Isabella to her room to read a book. I told Joshua that he needed to turn off his TV and read a book too. As I left that side of the house, I walked back over to the side of the house where I was working. Next on my list was wrapping presents to place under the tree, so I began working on that.

Standing in my dining room, I felt an urge to check on Josh. For the better part of sixteen years, I'd trained myself to listen to that voice almost exclusively. But, this morning, I didn't. I wanted to finish what I was doing. I didn't think I had room for distractions that day.

Ordinarily, I could sense Joshua's needs from anywhere in the house. His machines made certain noises when he was in distress, even in addition to the alarms that would go off. For instance, I could hear a slight change in the ebb and flow of his ventilator when he needed to be suctioned. My ears were trained to hear a whisper from him regardless of the level of chaos in the house. His survival depended on my instinct to know his needs. I was so internally focused that day and so incredibly tired, that I didn't hear his BiPap when it shut off.

Paul came home from running his errands and shouted, "What's wrong with him?" as he walked into Joshua's room. The panic in his voice sent me racing through the house. Joshua was ashen and gray. His eyes were shut. Paul was already on the other side of the bed assessing him.

I immediately said to turn the BiPap on. "It's broken," Paul said. I grabbed our back up from the closet and plugged it into the power strip. That one didn't work either. Panicked, I grabbed the Ambu bag. Paul, at this point, was administering CPR which was typically my responsibility. I sent Isabella to get our neighbor, Dr. Escobar. We called 911. I began moving things out of the way for the paramedics to have quick access to Josh. Dr Escobar appeared in the room and immediately took over CPR, and I administered the breaths with the Ambu bag. It felt like, on the most critical day, our roles in Joshua's care were reversed. We were both doing things that we typically didn't take the lead on. After sixteen years of doing

146

things the same way, we did things differently that day, and I have no idea why.

The paramedics arrived, and I gave them the report as they moved Joshua to the gurney. The team sent that day wasn't familiar with Joshua. We began discussing hospitals, and they said that they were taking him to Beaches Baptist. I begged them not to take him there, but they insisted due to his critical state. "We'll see you there," they said.

"No! You need me," I replied, with every ounce of fierce protectiveness that I possessed. I pushed through the crowd of people in my driveway and jumped into the ambulance alongside the paramedics. Finding my spot next to Joshua, and leaning over him, I began coaxing my son to stay with me. "You gotta do this, Joshie. You have to fight through this. You can't die today. C'mon baby, stay with me."

On the way to the hospital, I called Joshua's Pulmonologist on his cell phone. He was driving to the beach anyway and promised to meet me at the hospital. The paramedics worked on Joshua all the way to the hospital. He still had a pulse, so there was still hope. I couldn't give up hope, it was my constant anchor.

Upon arrival, we were greeted by, what appeared to be the newest resident doctor in the ER. Her body language told me that she was nervous. She couldn't intubate him. I felt so helpless there. I couldn't find control that day to save my life, more importantly, my son's. I wasn't in control of my brain to listen to the whisper. I wasn't in control in the room. I didn't assess the room as I normally would have. I wasn't in control at the ER, intubation was one of the few skills I never learned.

The Alison that I knew, the one I'd become over the years, didn't show up that day. She was too tired.

Dr. Shafer arrived and stood against the wall, looking into the room that we were in. I'd never known him to have any emotion, but that day he sobbed watching us fight for Joshua's life. Paul showed up as I walked out of the room to talk to our friends who'd come to the hospital. My best friend, Amy, was two weeks away from delivering her son. I remember begging her not to go into labor that day. I needed her. I went back into the room and continued praying for my son. They asked me to leave, so I moved to the doorway. I couldn't leave my son.

Time seemed to stand still. An eternity passed from the time that Paul shouted for me until they pronounced him dead at 12:30 p.m. The exact time of day that he entered the world fifteen years, ten months, and twenty-two days before.

The doctors and nurses filed out of the room one by one. Paul came in and I moved into his arms, sobbing. It seemed unfathomable that our son, laying on his left side so serenely in the hospital bed, could be dead. My son. The driving force behind every action of my day, dead? How could that be true? My heart knew it, even as my brain couldn't process it, and at some point, I collapsed on the sidewalk just outside the Emergency Room. I couldn't go on. I couldn't bear the thought of life without my green-eyed boy.

Later that day, I was laying in my son's bed, trying to smell him for the last time, when I noticed it.

The power strip was unplugged from the wall.

CHAPTER 25

GUILT

Alison

Everybody left two weeks later. His funeral was January 4, just after the holidays. Xanax and shock kept my head above water. I stopped taking the medicine shortly after we buried Joshua. I didn't like that it made me numb. I wanted to feel the pain. In fact, it was the only thing I wanted to feel. It kept me connected to Joshua.

My brain kept stressing over one single fact, the power strip wasn't plugged into the wall. How did I miss that? I was right there, face to face with it when I plugged the back-up BiPap into the power strip. But I missed it. I'm sure that it had already happened when I felt the urge to go check on my son that day, but I didn't. Instead of checking on him, I kept wrapping presents.

My son died, and it was my fault. I should feel pain. I deserved to feel the pain. It didn't matter that I figured out quickly how the power strip came unplugged or that there was another person involved. My brain wasn't concerned with logic; he was my responsibility, and I failed. It didn't matter that I couldn't possibly have known at the time, I should have known, or that's what I told myself. To this day, the person responsible does not know as it would not change anything. Why destroy another person's life with this guilt? We couldn't turn back time. It was an accident.

I'd spent the week before he died gallivanting around New York with my daughter. I desperately wished I could change that week. If I'd known his life could be measured in days, I wouldn't have left his side. He called me while I was there and said, "Mom, I miss you." We flew home the next day, but still I wish I'd never gone.

I slid into depression the likes of which I'd never known before. It was such a deep, dark place in my brain. And I wanted to be there. I didn't have the energy to be in public with my grief on display. Or, worse, hidden. My world was forever shattered. To pretend otherwise, even if just while purchasing groceries, was incomprehensible to me. I withdrew from society almost entirely. I didn't want anybody pulling me out of my dark hole. I felt connected to him there. As if by suffering, I would know how he suffered at the end.

Guilt over my son's death threatens to suffocate me. To this day, when I think about the day he died, the strongest parts of the story—the parts my brain emphasizes—are all the parts that I could've changed. I should've noticed that Paul took his oximeter off when I separated the kids. It would've had me checking all of his machines. I should've checked on him when I felt the nudge. I should've seen the power cord. Those moments combine into one deafening roar: "It's my fault my son died." I wasn't in my A-game. I could've saved him.

Paul feels the same way, naturally. He sees the list of things that he could've done differently. We seldom talk about it; the guilt is too intense. Isabella isn't immune to it either. Years after Joshua passed, she told me that she felt responsible for his death. I couldn't believe my ears! How could a nine-year-old carry that burden? Through tears, she told me that if she hadn't argued with him, then she wouldn't have been sent to her room. If she hadn't been sent to her room, then she would've been there when he began having trouble breathing. She could've been his alarm when his machines failed to alarm me.

Preposterous.

"That's not yours to carry," I told her. I repeated what my spiritual advisor said to me as I wrestled through Joshua's death, "God is sovereign, even in death." If that's true, then it would stand to reason that it's preposterous to blame myself for his death too. I wish my heart would believe that.

CHAPTER 26

FOUR WEEKS AFTER DEATH

Paul

Joshua had been gone for over a month. Alison, Isabella, and I were dealing with the pain, each in our own way. I, personally, was not dealing with things well. Pain faded and was replaced with numbness and at times darkness.

It was late January, and I needed to go for a run.

I mapped out a route that started at the parking lot under the bridge that spanned the intercostal waterway (ICW) in a part of town called Palm Valley. The ICW was only a couple of miles, as the crow flies, from the ocean at this location in Ponte Vedra Beach, Florida.

I had the distance of runs over the bridge measured at two, three, four and a half, and six miles. I'd choose a distance depending on the day and how I felt. I started this run with three miles stuck in my head. The three-mile course would take me up and over the Palm Valley bridge, and then another two-thirds of a mile to the red light at the turn for the Ponte Vedra High School and Davis Park, the local municipal park that had numerous soccer, baseball, and football fields for recreation. I was feeling pretty good as I approached the light, and I decided to take the left and head toward the high school. Four-tenths of a mile and I found myself leaning against the chain-link fence, staring across the retention pond at the school Joshua had attended for the last year and a half. I'd driven to and from this exact location for the last two school years, up until December 23, 2010.

I turned to start the jog back, but I felt an urge to jog down the right side of the school and visit the drop off location where I'd unloaded and loaded Joshua, in and out of the van, twice a day for the last two school years. This was the first time I'd been back since Joshua's death. As I jogged around the west side of the school, I looked over my right shoulder into the pine grove which must have been harvested and replanted around twenty-five years before. Time changes a lot of things. The field was barren twenty-five years before, but it had forty-foot pine trees on it now. I wondered, would the passing of time ever change the way Alison, Isabella, and I were feeling? I began to think of Joshua more and more. I reached the door to the school and looked south. Beyond the parking lot were a few volleyball courts with basketball hoops at the base lines, and beyond them, a quarter-mile track surrounding a practice field. At any given time, there would be student athletes on the fields, practicing lacrosse, soccer, field and track, or football. It was just before 5 p.m. and the fields were empty. Empty; a feeling that had become all too familiar. I had been feeling very numb for quite some time, and I didn't want to feel that way.

I turned back and faced the door I'd entered and exited hundreds of times. I reached for the handle; was it unlocked? I pressed down on the latch and found myself opening the door and walking into the school. I started to walk down the hallway toward Joshua's room. This hallway covered the entire width of the west wing of the school. I walked straight ahead for fifty yards or so. The hallway felt like a long tunnel. As I walked slowly toward Joshua's room, I started to reminisce about all the times I had raced down the hallway with Isabella, in a competition to see who could reach Joshua first. I took a left at the end of the hall, and walked for another ten yards, remembering the sound of Isabella's voice bouncing off the walls of the empty hallway. I don't ever remember an echo, but today, I heard Isabella's voice echoing, "I'm going to beat you, Daddy. Hurry up, let's go see Josh! Come on, Daddy; hurry up; let's go!" I would probably never run down this hallway again with Isabella or hear her voice echoing off the walls and hard tiled floor. Joshua's room was on the right. This door was usually locked, so I was surprised to find the lever moved freely.

I pulled the door open, and the light automatically turned on. I had never noticed that they had it on a motion sensor. I walked to the back left of the room and stood there, staring at the wire basket that held Joshua's books. I pictured Joshua's slant board standing with one of his books open and waiting for us to study. Joshua's teachers hadn't moved a thing. This was the corner where Joshua and Linda would park his gurney and do his homework. Hundreds of hours had been spent in this corner. His table was still there. So was a red metal wagon filled with agility drill equipment where Joshua's gurney used to be. Coach Gordy had shared this room with Joshua. Gordon was a large, gregarious man with an even bigger heart who'd played college football. Now, he was a teacher for special education kids and a football coach at the high school. Just a month before Josh died, I had a business trip that took me to Orlando for two days. Coach Gordy helped Alison and Nurse Linny lift Joshua in and out of the van on those days. He was a good friend of Joshua's and would say he felt bad for Joshua, knowing that his wife, Mrs. Rolison, was Joshua's first period English teacher. They enjoyed a fun *man to man* relationship. Coach Gordy treated Joshua like one of the guys, locker room talk and all. Joshua really enjoyed that.

Something was missing. I turned to my right and looked across the room. The gurney was pushed against the wall. I slowly walked over while trying to picture Joshua on it. Memories of racing Joshua down the hall after school, when no kids were there, came flooding in. Joshua would be yelling, "Linda, Linda, make him stop," and I'd take a pit stop to see how many times and how fast I could spin Joshua in a circle without bouncing him off one of the walls. "Stop dad, stop!" He and I would always be dizzy after one of these scenes, and there are a few marks on the wall that prove my lack of judgment as I spun him around and around.

As I approached his gurney, all the sheets and blankets had been pulled off, and the egg carton foam pads lay bare on top of the bed. His neoprene pillow had been stripped and was lying on top of the foam pad. I leaned against the rail of the bed and looked down at his pillow. I placed my hand on his pillow. I began to feel a knot in my throat as I tried to picture Joshua's head on the pillow. The foam was surrounding my hand as I pressed down. I pulled my hand away and the impression of my hand remained for a few seconds. I pictured Joshua's head and neck leaving an impression on the pillow. The tears began to flow. I knew there were security cameras all over, but I was facing the wall; they couldn't see my face. Besides, I didn't care. I began to breathe deep and hard, trying to suppress the tears. I couldn't. They were destined to come. My shoulders began to heave as the sobs became uncontrollable. I hadn't cried since Christmas day, less than thirty-six hours after Joshua died so suddenly. I kept pressing my hand into the pillow and imagining my son's head resting peacefully. I longed to run my fingers through his hair. I yearned to rub his back. I ached to hug his body. I wanted, so desperately, to kiss his cheek one more time.

I cried for a while and then let myself into the bathroom just a few steps to the left of Joshua's bed to get some paper towels to dry my tears. I returned to the gurney, and I placed my hand on his pillow one more time. I could not avoid the pain of losing my son. I could not avoid the emptiness, and I could not come to terms with the void, the gaping hole that was left by his absence. Would the pain ever subside?

I walked out the door to the front of the school. I pictured days gone by when I had pushed and pulled Joshua through that school on his gurney. I remembered sitting with Joshua in his classes when nurse Linny was detained because of responsibilities or illness. Like the echoing of Isabella's voice through those empty halls, these things would never happen again.

As I walked toward the front of the school, I felt relieved. I felt a heaviness lift off my chest. It was good to cry. It was good to remember. Alison was just telling me the day before that she was worried about me, that I hadn't cried about Joshua, that I was holding it all in. She'd expressed her concern about me *stuffing* these emotions and them coming out later in an unhealthy manner, through an emotional explosion, or maybe even an illness. The manifestations could be in many ways, but the end result would be the same, unnecessary pain and suffering. It felt good to let it out; it was good to let it go; and I felt comfort in *letting it be*. This was essential for the healing to begin.

CHAPTER 27

THE WHOLE TRUTH

Paul

I am a married man. Here, in America, that means I have a 50% chance of my marriage ending in divorce. I am the father of a child with special needs. Parents of children with special needs have an 80% chance that their marriage will end in divorce. I am also a retired NFL player which gives me a 60-80% chance that my marriage will end in divorce. When Joshua passed away, I became the father of a deceased child which carries a 75% chance that my marriage will end in divorce.

Marriage, in general, is hard, or so I've heard. Alison and I have never experienced the luxury of a normal marriage, not even before Joshua was born. The NFL makes it effortless to live at the surface of life. While I'm sure that we had disagreements the first few years, there was enough money to buy rose-colored glasses and tensions seldom rose. The moment Joshua was born, we knew our lives would never be the same. But I didn't know the scope of our new reality would also encompass our marriage. Of course, we didn't mean for it to happen, but by the time we realized it was happening, it was almost too late.

There's a dichotomy in marriage when you're faced with life-altering trauma. You are married to the only person on the face of the planet that knows exactly what you're walking through, but at the same time, you're alone in your grief. While I know Alison's life with Joshua inside and out, she is the only one who loved him with a mother's love, and who grieves for him with a mother's heart. Likewise, Alison can never truly know and experience my journey as Joshua's father. Our parallel lives began in the NICU.

When Joshua was born and we were told that he might not survive the day, we were devastated. I stood there numb and unresponsive as Alison wept. While Alison was resting in the recovery room, I stood at the window of the neonatal intensive care unit and watched a doctor and two nurses working on my son. I didn't feel pain, anguish, or fear; I just stood there watching, feeling numb.

Alison and I both went into survival mode which meant something drastically different for each of us. I went into the mode of, "I'll do whatever it takes to get through this successfully. Just give me instructions and I will follow them to a T." Alison, on the other hand, realized quickly that these doctors, as good as they were, had no clue what Joshua was afflicted with. They were just testing out theories on how to care for him. She kicked into action immediately and politely but firmly began making suggestions regarding Joshua's care. In the midst of the chaos of the NIC unit, I would steal away and quietly connect with my son. I would sit next to his bed and drape myself over his body, whispering in his ear, and staring into his eyes.

Those early years with Josh were hard for us in different ways. Alison shouldered the burden of Joshua's daily care while also fighting for medical coverage, not to mention starting the foundation. I, on the other hand, struggled to stay intensely focused on the game while also supporting my wife long distance. Being in Green Bay was the hardest. It was the height of my career, and I was in an emotional vacuum. My choices off the field were to sit by myself in the sparse apartment I refused to furnish and think about the life I was missing 1,200 miles away or head to the local Mexican restaurant with Jeff Thomason for nachos and a few beers. The twenty-seven pounds I gained there didn't hold a candle to the weight I felt when I couldn't see Joshua for five months.

Ultimately, I was absent twenty-eight out of the first forty-eight months while I played out my career. I returned home to a woman I didn't recognize. The vivacious woman I married had withered away to a shell of what once was. She was physically, mentally, and emotionally drained. I'm sure there were moments Alison dreamed of a one-way ticket to anywhere but home. It took me a few years to truly understand how difficult it was and how near she actually was to a total breakdown.

I don't believe anyone retires from football on their own terms…. If I were physically still able to play today, I probably would. After I was asked to leave the game, I struggled with how to take care of my family financially, as well as emotionally. We had a small nest egg that I knew would eventually run out, so I had to figure out how to make a living with my psychology degree. I fumbled my way through a few different professions without experiencing enough success to fully provide for our needs. Adding financial stress to an already stressful life quickly became a leading point of contention for us.

It didn't take long for me to learn what it truly meant to be involved in Joshua's daily care. I had only been home a few weeks before Alison had to revive our son in his own bed and continuously use the Ambu bag until the EMTs arrived to give her a brief spell. I can't even explain the adrenaline rush you feel when you are fighting for the life of your son, and you know his life is hanging in the balance. It's not the exhilarating rush you get when your blood runs through your veins and you feel flush in your face, down your neck, and throughout your whole body. It's not the same as when you get ready for the contest, or the rush of energy you get when you sack Dan Marino, and you dance around like a fool in front of screaming fans.

It's an adrenaline rush like no other. Instead of your blood rushing, you are filled with a calming dread. The blood rushes out of your face and you become pale and dazed, but woefully focused on what is taking place. I remember watching Alison during these times, and I liken her to a pilot who has ice in their veins; always calm and calculated while under great pressure. As I mentioned above, I was an executor; tell me what to do, and I'll do it with excellence. Alison had the ability to give instructions while carrying out tasks at the same time, and fortunately for our family, her directives saved our son's life many times.

From the beginning, Alison and I knew how to operate as teammates in Joshua's care. For all our differences, we managed to find a way to complement each other. If Alison was the coach, I was an excellent quarterback. She ran the foundation while I became our public face. We struggled with health insurance and what they would pay and would not pay. She negotiated rates, filed all the insurance claims, and worked hand in hand with the NFL. Everything in our life rotated around Joshua, his care, and the hope of a cure. Somewhere in the middle of those formative years with Joshua, our marriage—already operating on parallel planes—faded into the background. Alison and I only left the house as a couple twice a year at the most, and sometimes only during our annual fundraiser in Boston when we'd leave Joshua with his band of nurses for no more than three to five days at a time. More than once we had to cut a short trip even shorter and rush home to meet Joshua and the nurses in the hospital.

We struggled with the decision to not put Joshua on permanent life support for a myriad of reasons. Even though he'd never needed it, there might come a time when he would. I had deep discussions with Alison and multiple friends about the issue, and the question always arose, "Are you preserving life, or are you delaying death?"

These conversations continued throughout Joshua's life, and eventually he was even able to participate in them. Joshua was adamant that he did not want to lose his voice. We knew that we would never be able to *pull the plug* if we had to make that decision, but who in their right mind ever thinks or plans ahead for that event? Well, parents like us, if they were being real, always asked and tried to answer these questions. That was our *normal*. And it sucked, (excuse me; was less than desirable).

We got into a routine, but Alison was weary, and I was in more of a rut than a routine. I'd been eroding for years on the inside, and my walls were about to crumble. I struggled with our situation, Joshua, our finances, the lack of a life we had, and the lack of marital bliss that we both fully anticipated when we got married. We were so focused on survival, that we neglected to cultivate the marriage. Had we worked on our marriage along the way, it might not have suffered the way it did. However, there's only so much time in a day, and when every ounce of strength is given to keeping your son alive and your family afloat it doesn't leave much energy left over to devote to nurturing a relationship with your spouse. In fact, any spare time I had was devoted to finding an escape from my reality.

I began, slowly at first, to indulge in a beer or two after work. This wouldn't typically be a problem except I drank it by the quart. Over time, one or two turned into five or six…nightly. On top of all of our struggles,

I added a self-induced struggle to the mix, and it helped to erode what little relationship Alison and I had left. Again, as it had taken me a while to realize the impact of things on Alison during those early years with Joshua, it took me a few years to fully understand the implications of my choices regarding my lack of temperance. If we thought life was stressful before, it was about to take a turn for the worse.

When Joshua was born, I had benefits through the NFL, and Gene Upshaw and the Players Association opted to raise the maximum individual benefits two times during our time on the plan. The plan went from a $1 million lifetime cap to a $2.5 million maximum because of Joshua. We were immensely grateful for their generosity and the carte blanche freedom we had to care for Joshua. We ran up against that cap just as my Cobra policy was ending. Now we were going to experience what a true group plan was like. Initially, we faired fairly well as the company we joined, AvMed, had home healthcare. We used them at their max: sixteen hours a day. A nurse came for four hours after school, and the twelve at night allowed us to sleep well and get the energy needed to face another day. The battle really began when they jumped through hoops and *legally* altered the home health care portion of their policy to allow for only forty, four-hour visits per year. So, we went from a possible 8,760 hours of coverage annually, of which we only used approximately 4,300 hours, because we didn't want to run through our new cap, nor abuse the situation, down to 160 hours, PER YEAR. Then the insurance company decided they would not cover our annual visits. Alison went right to the top of the Office of Insurance Regulations (OIR), and she filed the complaint. She was given the lead counsel of OIR to oversee this investigation. In the end, the insurance company and OIR were in bed together.

Alison's decision came to a halt. "Do we really have the time and money to take on an insurance company in addition to caring for Joshua?"

We spent our own money at $48 per hour for about a year and a half, and when the money was near its end, I became Joshua's night nurse. This is when my downward spiral really accelerated.

My routine for just over four years was night nurse from roughly 8:00 p.m. until dropping Joshua off at school by 8:30 a.m., while trying to work a full-time job, all on three to five hours of broken sleep per night, weekends too. As any mother with a newborn can tell you, sleep deprivation is a monster. In fact, sleep deprivation is one of the tools used to garner confessions from hardened criminals. So, if life with a child constantly staving off death, a bank account on the verge of depletion, and a prolific drinking career didn't bring us to rock bottom, sleep deprivation did. I became tired, ornery, and for the first time, deeply resentful.

In Alison's defense, Joshua was too big and heavy for her to carry with her residual back injury from the car accident in '91. This was the first time since Joshua was born that I began to say, "Why me?" I can tell you that even when I said it, I felt like a heel, because I'd never heard my son, not even once, utter words like that, and he was the one in the wheelchair, fighting for every breath he took.

I began to resent that I was the only one who could physically care for Joshua. I was the one who stayed home when Alison and Bella went skiing or to New York over Christmas break or to Maine in the summer months. I wanted Alison to do these things with Bella to give her a break, and to give Isabella the experiences, but deep down inside, I was going to a dark and resentful place, a place where I never want to return. My personal demons began to haunt me. I would pull into the municipal park a mile from our home, and I'd watch the young kids play football and baseball, and I started to wonder what it would have been like if Joshua had been healthy. Would he have been a Little League All-star like his old man was? Would he have wanted to play football? What would life have been like if, if, if...

Joshua had called me out for drinking too much. I tried hard to quit, for him. I also had a very sobering experience with my daughter Isabella a year after our trip to DC. By this time in my drinking life, I'd been desperately trying to stop for well over a year. This evening was just like many before. I'd started my trip home from work with good intentions but failed miserably along the way.

Bella was in a fishing phase, and we'd bought her a fishing pole for her birthday. It was common for her to ask me to take her to the little retention pond near our house so that she could throw a line in for a few minutes.

I walked in the door feeling like a failure, ready to face my family and my son once again while trying to cover up the obvious. The second I walked through that door, Bella yelled, "Daddy, let's go fishing." Alison could already tell I'd been drinking, but she ignored me, so I turned and started to follow my little girl to the pond across the street. I baited her hook, and I sat down behind Isabella and leaned my back against a tree and proceeded to watch my daughter cast. I was feeling downright depressed that I'd found myself in this situation again.

I lost myself in thought as Bella cast line after line in the water. Back in those days, Bella dreamed of catching fish. It was all she talked about. Watching Bella cast, it occurred to me that she was going after what she wanted; she was chasing her dream. I felt the tears well up in my eyes, and my throat became tight and dry. Right there, leaning against that tree, watching my precious, beautiful daughter casting for her dreams, I asked myself, "What happened to my dreams?"

Feeling so down on myself, I began to cry like a baby. I was bawling my eyes out silently with shoulders heaving. I didn't want Bella to notice. She cast a few more times as I gained my composure then turned to me and said, "Let's go see Josh, Daddy!" I got up and followed her home to see Joshua and Alison, both broken hearted once again that daddy and husband had been drinking.

The next year and a half or so, I went through a phase where I'd string a few months together not drinking, and then I'd drink for a week or two, and then go another month without it, and so on. I finally got a fairly strong hold on it in June of 2010, and I remained alcohol free for the next ten months. I know, without a shadow of a doubt, that if I had been in my drinking mode when Joshua passed away, the guilt would have consumed me beyond my ability to handle it.

If I were a betting man, I wouldn't bet on my marriage. The odds simply aren't in our favor. Our marriage has suffered greatly but our story as man and wife isn't finished quite yet. It goes without saying that this particular aspect of marriage isn't often on public display, and I wouldn't talk about it now, if not for the sneaky suspicion that I am not alone. As parents, we were on a mission to keep our son alive. Our dedication toward that goal came with tremendous sacrifice. Over the years, Alison and I have lost ourselves and struggled to find ourselves. Our marriage, pummeled by life, absorbed all the blows along the way.

I will not allow my story to be that of a man brought to his knees by Myotubular Myopathy. I have the rest of my life ahead of me, and I am determined for it to be a healthy one.

CHAPTER 28

THE BIRTHDAY PRESENT

Paul

Alan Beggs told Alison about the conference in October of 2011. The conference was to be held in New Orleans, sometime in June. Alison was reluctant to commit as she had just attended a five-day conference in Washington, DC a few months before. In her mind, this would be the same format, and quite frankly, she didn't feel she had enough value to add that would warrant five days away from Isabella when summer activities were just getting started. Not to mention the fact that we were still reeling from the loss of Joshua, and the simple act of living an ordinary life was incredibly difficult. She told Alan she'd think about it.

In the following days, Anne Rutowski (founder of Cure Congenital Muscular Disease—Cure CMD) and Alison began envisioning taking advantage of having all these researchers and PhDs in one location and adding JFF and Cure CMD content to the itinerary. As they wrapped their heads around it, the event morphed from a biology of skeletal muscle for congenital myopathies to discussing protocol to get these sciences to clinical trials. Alison was starting to warm up to the idea but was not sold that we could pull it off. It was a daunting task that would take all hands-on deck, and Alison was grieving. She couldn't fathom how they could do it. Alison asked Anne what date the conference fell on. Anne said, "June 17," Alison's birthday.

Through the years of administering 24/7 care for our son, there were times when we both became weary. Many times, this weariness was exponentially greater for Alison. She expended massive energy every time she had to revive Joshua and take him to the hospital, which included training and coercing any new docs on duty on how to care for our son. In addition to that, she also helped families from across the world, guiding them through their journey of birth, life, crisis, and death. The initial fifty children with MTM when Joshua was born is now several hundred, most of whom Alison knows personally.

The emotional roller coaster had incredible peaks of jubilation and valleys of despair, and the energy it took to sustain the uphill battle was frequently depleted. Her tank was empty and there were no *filling stations* in sight. A few times over the years, Alison would slump in exhaustion and beg God for wisdom and strength. With her emotional, physical, and spiritual tanks tapped, the outflow far exceeded the intake, and she would cry out for relief and a sign, could she go on? Should she go on with the foundation and its direction? How could she possibly not go on? She was fighting for our son and the Joshuas of the world. Often, these were the same moments that she would realize that she was right where she was supposed to be, and although at times it didn't seem like it, she knew she was being guided and sustained. Those moments were miraculous, and we believe orchestrated.

Alison's birthday present was a resounding message that she should go to this conference and take full advantage of the plan that was unfolding. Alison and Anne went to work and planned two very important meetings. Both meetings proved to be the springboard for many orphan disease groups to band together and collaborate. Often, this collaboration leads to potential cures for these diseases being brought to clinical trial as their respective sciences advance. This was all about saving lives.

Alison planned to make the trip alone until months later when she realized that June 17, 2012, was also Father's Day. Alison knew that there was not a more fitting situation, than to be together celebrating her birthday and Father's Day, while having a *round table discussion* with scientists from all over the world on how to initiate clinical trials and start saving the lives of Joshua's peers. We had never allowed ourselves to think so far ahead, because until just eight months before, we were still simply hoping our science would work.

The stage was set.

June 16, 2012 finally arrived. We had anticipated this day for the last three months. As we boarded the plane, Alison answered a call from her niece, Amanda. I overheard Alison tell her that we were going to New Orleans and that she'd never been before, but I'd played in the Sugar Bowl there about fifty years ago. Not funny.

As the plane carried us to Louis Armstrong New Orleans International Airport, Alison and I went over last-minute details. We reviewed the list of attendees and the itinerary. I began to review the U34 application that Casey had worked on which led to a discussion of what we were embarking on this weekend. We experienced many emotions: disbelief, amazement, excitement, and anxiousness. We were stepping into the unknown, but it was the unknown that we had searched for years. The unknown that would have saved our Joshua; the unknown that will now save his peers. It was beautiful and wonderful and slightly scary. We landed and grabbed a cab to the hotel.

As we checked into the hotel, we ran into Rob Grange, our research scientist from Virginia Tech, along with his graduate assistant, John. We invited them to dinner and promptly began to barrage them with questions about the research.

Alan Beggs and Casey Childers arrived at the hotel about 10:30 p.m. and I met them at the hotel bar to say hello and visit for a few moments. Alan was absolutely beaming when I walked up to him. He was not usually this animated. He pulled me close and said, "Can you believe that we are all here to talk about frickin' clinical trials?" I had never heard a word like this out of our lead scientist's mouth! Alan was pumped up for these meetings. The atmosphere kind of felt like the locker room I was in with the Green Bay Packers during the 1997 NFC playoffs. A controlled fury was brewing, and nothing could stop it. The only thing that could temper it was the referee, and at that moment, in New Orleans, the referee arrived. Carsten Bonneman joined us.

Carsten is an accomplished scientist, as are Alan and Casey. Carsten's appointment up until eighteen months prior was with the Children's Hospital of Philadelphia (referred to by all scientists as CHOPS), which was associated with the Ivy League school, the University of Pennsylvania (UPENN). Carsten was currently with the National Institutes of Health

(NIH). The NIH was the referee, the line judge, and the umpire when it came to monitoring and funding scientific research. Carsten was here for the conference, and he was a friend of Alan and Casey. He had seen Casey present our science before and was very impressed. We had invited him to consult with us as we traversed new territory, planning a clinical trial. It was time for me to say goodnight, so I said my goodbyes and excused myself. I let myself quietly into the room; Alison was asleep.

I awoke early the next morning and started getting ready for the meeting. I was showered and dressed by the time Alison woke up, around 6:45 a.m. I wished her Happy Birthday, and she reciprocated with Happy Father's Day. She sat up to read the card I had handed her. We shared a few moments thinking of Joshua, mourning, laughing, and crying. We thought about 0 in New York, and about Bella in Florida. We dared to think about a cure and about saving lives, all because of a boy named Joshua.

I wanted to get down to the room and make sure everything was set. When I got down to the twelfth floor, Gregory met me, the gentlemen who Alison had been speaking with the last month or so, orchestrating the correct setup for the room. With JFF behind it, it had to be perfect. Everything was in working order and set up correctly. It was around 7:45 a.m., and I knew our scientists would start trickling in. The first person to arrive was Casey Childers, then Rob Grange with his assistant John. Jim Dowling from the University of Michigan entered the room, followed by Carsten Bonneman, and then Alison. Alan strolled in shortly after Alison. He dropped his bag and gave Alison a big hug. Alison and I heard the French accent coming from outside of the room. We had waited for this moment for a long time. We were about to meet Anna Buj-Bello from France. Anna was working under Mandel and with Jocelyn Laporte when Dr. Laporte found and cloned the gene for Myotubular Myopathy. Anna dedicated her life to researching our son's disorder and her name had been on just about every paper that Alan had written since we'd been funding Boston Children's Hospital. The opportunity to meet her face-to-face was a real honor. She rounded the corner and came through the door. A number of our scientists know her and exchanged greetings with the French double cheek touch: right cheek to right cheek and then left to left. Alison and I approached her, and Alan introduced us as the Frases. She looked at us as though she was just as glad to be meeting us as we were to meet her. Alison reached out to shake her hand and Anna proceeded with the cheek-to-cheek greeting. The first thing Anna said to us was that she was sorry that the research had not progressed fast enough to save our Joshua. As a mother of three, Anna connected immediately with Alison, and it was the beginning of a wonderful encounter.

Marsha, from the University of Washington joined us, and we all grabbed coffee and some fruit and sat down to begin the meeting. Anne Rutkowski joined us via phone conference from Denmark. She was finishing up a conference at which she was able to meet the Denmark MDA and make some alliances. It was time to get to the business at hand. We needed a plan to save the lives of Joshua's peers, first through clinical trials. We weren't long into the meeting before we realized why Alan was so excited to be there. He'd seen the video Casey was about to show us.

CHAPTER 29

BEAUTY FOR ASHES

Alison

I'm sitting in my office; stacks of paperwork surround me despite my best efforts to keep a clean desk. It's a bright, sunny day in north Florida. Tears stream down my cheeks as I tap out an email to a mom halfway across the country. She's sitting in PICU watching her son battle for his life. We email back and forth a few more times until the mom can sneak away and call me. I move from the office to my living room and find a seat in my favorite yellow chair. It's where I have all my important conversations. I listen as she struggles through the options, and then I do for her what my mom did for me, I give her my strength. Words of determination are coated in empathy as I give her my fighting spirit. I spent sixteen years advocating for my son, and I teach other moms how to do the same. We hang up, and from the corner of my eye, I catch a glimpse of the snapshot somebody took of Joshua and me on his very first day of school, and I crumple into a pile of tears. He was so full of joy.

This is my reality, my day in and day out. Seldom are tears more than a stone's throw away. For years, I would lay in bed at night, so exhausted from the day that I could barely function, and in those moments of quiet, give in to the tears I'd managed to hold at bay during the day. That's what this disorder does to you; it strips you bare and then puts your deepest fear on public display. The morning Joshua died, my deepest fear, the one born with his first breath, became my reality.

C.S. Lewis once wrote, "The greater the love, the greater the grief." Tears aren't just a by-product of this journey, they are the price of love, and

I've never fallen so deeply in love as I did the day that I looked into those big green eyes for the first time. I told him that once. He was lying on his bed, and I was leaning over him, kissing him goodnight. I'd told him thousands of times before, but it is a mother's right to repeat this over and over. "I love you, Joshie," I said.

"I love you too," he replied.

Grabbing the chance to make it a game, I shot back, "But I love you more!"

"No!" he said, "I love YOU more!"

"But," I countered, "I've loved you since before you were born."

Never one to lose an argument, he thought for a moment then said, "I loved you when I was in your belly. I just couldn't see your face yet." Who am I to argue with that?

Loving Joshua cost me just about everything I had. Not only did MTM rob me of any semblance of a normal life, but it also robbed me of my dreams. Aside from the painfully obvious parts of my story, the crushing sorrow that comes from the death of dreams is what almost did me in. Grief, in the world of special needs, is an ongoing reality. Grief is messy. It's uncomfortable. It's running to your car after you leave the fertility doctor just nodding your head as he refused your case because at thirty-six with one special needs kid at home, you're too "high risk." Adding insult to injury, you refuse to have an abortion should you become pregnant with another boy. It's hot tears streaming down your face and white knuckles from your death grip on the wheel, because you just came face to face with the reality that the last fertile years of your life were spent fighting for the life of your son, and you'll never get the big family you dreamed of as a kid.

It's looking out the window as streams of mothers pass by on their beach cruisers with their perfectly healthy baby strapped to the back, wiping away tears as you push more food through the syringe and into the tube coming out of your son's side, wishing ever so desperately that you could be one of those mothers. It's sitting at a table in the middle of a restaurant, dressed up to meet your friends, surrounded by noise…but clothed in silence. Stories fly across the table, each mother sharing her latest adventures with the kids, every story better than the last, and knowing that you have nothing to share. Who can take grand adventures when every breath is a battle? It's slipping farther and farther into the background, until eventually you just stop showing up to those lunches.

Living with grief becomes the new normal. It grows with you and changes over time. It tracks healthy kids your son's age and highlights all the moments that will never be: crawling, taking his first step into your arms, running around playing superheroes in the backyard, learning to ride a bike without training wheels, walking into kindergarten and sitting at a desk, watching him leave for prom, walk across the stage to graduate, kiss his bride for the first time, and become a dad. These moments strike like a quick unexpected blow, and they demand to be noticed. But it's also just life. Our will to survive is stronger than our grief, and so we've learned to function within the sorrow. We've learned to find a safe place to give in to the tears and then wipe them away with a smile on our face, focusing on what's right in front of us; our beautifully perfect child.

Pain invites us to grow, and it always comes with choices: we can live in the ashes that life hands us, or we can revel in the beauty all around us. Twenty years ago, I made a conscious decision to do the latter. I made a promise to Joshua that we would fully embrace this one wild and precious life we had together, and we did. I knew he would never have a lot of friends, so I wanted his world to be full of laughter, and it was. Josh was born with a wry sense of humor, and we explored every part of it. We played games, made up stories about the people and places around us. We became a comedy group; he would tell me what to do, and I would execute it. Once, we found a stuffed rat, and he would tell me where to hide it to get the best scare out of his grandma Rockett. His body was broken, but his mind was sharp as a tack, so we explored the universe from his spot on the bed. We used what we could see and touch. We built cities out of Legos, studied everything we could get our hands on about WWII; he knew every detail about anything he found interest in. Planes? He could tell you ever detail about any aircraft in WWII and exactly which country flew it. We made the best with what we had, and it was wonderful.

I could have focused on what was lost, but then I would meet a parent whose situation was far worse than mine and I would remind myself I didn't have it that bad. Joshua could tell me that he loved me. We could talk to each other. What a gift! Josh couldn't walk but he could sit in a wheelchair and wheelchairs can go places! We took that kid everywhere. When he couldn't sit up in a wheelchair anymore, we found a wagon. And, you know what?

When your friend calls and says, "Hey, do you want to go out on a boat?" You don't need either. A cushion laid on the seat will do the trick. We only intended to be on the boat for fifteen minutes that day, but the weather was perfect, and he had that Rockett blood in him that craves salty-sea air.

An hour later at the opening of the intercostal, we found a perfect island to wade out on. We looked at each other and I said, "Josh, do you want to be adventurous?" He loved adventure. Paul picked him up and carried him to shore, and we spent three hours lying on the beach in front of tidal pools watching creation move around us. Joshua was experiencing the essence of my childhood.

On the way home, perched in the bow, he looked at me and said, "Mom, this is the best day of my life." Twelve years later, it's still one of my favorite memories.

It would be easy to focus on the loss of my dream to have a large family, but then I would have missed the miracle of conceiving our daughter, Isabella, just two months after being rejected by that fertility doctor. At sixteen weeks, when we had her sonogram, she was sitting up in my uterus, knees folded underneath her, and facing the camera. She raised one hand up and waved right at us, and Paul and I crumpled into a pile of tears. She was going to be okay. Josh spent the next six months putting his hand on my belly, hoping to feel a kick, while we talked about how he was going to be the best big brother ever. His excitement knew no limits when it came time to meet his sister.

I was overdue and the doctors were scheduling an induction. I ironed his outfit and laid it out for the nurses. My mom and I experimented with all the old wives' tales, trying to do anything to get Isabella out. Two days later, Isabella was here and Josh came to meet her the next day. Paul held her in front of him, and Joshua leaned in to look, one arm propping his head up so he didn't flop forward. He stared at her in amazement. Those big eyes of his filled with adoration as he took in every ounce of her. There was an instant connection between them, a bond that would go deeper than

I could've dreamed possible, even if he did ask to, "Send her back," two weeks later when he felt like I was spending too much time with her.

Isabella was born the opposite of Joshua. She never stopped moving. It was as if she knew that my heart needed to see her strength, so as a newborn she could hold her head up and look around. If she was in the room with us, she was content. She adored her big brother and became his sidekick until the day he died. My first Mother's Day after Isabella was born, Paul bought me a pink beach cruiser with a child seat attached to the back. We went on bike rides as often as possible. To this day, that is the most meaningful gift I've ever received. I still have that bike twenty years later.

Joshua changed the course of my life. He introduced me to a new way of living, and a new way of thinking about things. His disorder brought me to the door of some of the best researchers in the country—men and women who have dedicated their professional careers to finding cures for children with rare diseases. It's because of Joshua that we found ourselves in a community of families with neuromuscular disorders, and my life is richer for it. By no means is it an accident that I get to walk with a mom across the country as she navigates a PICU for the first time; it is because of Joshua. And, while it might cause tears, it is a great honor to me that I have the privilege of walking this journey with her. My life is filled with hundreds of kids I adore, parents who continually amaze me, friends who share in the triumph and the grief that comes with this disorder, and researchers racing toward a cure.

It's easy to pause by the door to Joshua's old room, to look at his model cars set up so perfectly on the shelf and let waves of grief flood over me. I miss him every moment of my day. How could I not? But then, I look around and I see that he's everywhere. He lived a great big life in a tiny little broken body, and its reach knew no bounds. He's interwoven in the core of our family, his touch threading between Paul, Isabella, and I, living in the memories and stories we tell, creating a separate, unique bond between us. We knew Josh, he knew us, and we are better for it. We live in the profoundness of that statement. We knew great love. And now we know great loss. But all is not lost. We had him for fifteen years, ten months, and twenty-two days, and we packed a lifetime of memories into those years. I am the woman I am because he lived. I could look at the ashes, but then I would miss the beauty of who Joshua was.

CHAPTER 30

THE PATH TO VENTURE CAPITAL BEGINS
Paul

In 2010, Alison and I began to discuss the importance of wrapping intellectual property around our science. We knew it was paramount and we began to pepper our scientists with questions about the intellectual property they believed was in our science. Our goal as a Foundation was to perpetuate funding to our scientists to tackle new diseases. With the scientific advancement of gene transfer and gene replacement therapies and protein fusion therapy, we felt we could create a financial model that would allow for a continuous flow of funding from previous orphan disease research successes; MTM hopefully proving to be the first. We could see the potential to attack some of the more than 7,000 genetic disorders which affected one in ten people across the US, one at time. There are approximately thirty million people afflicted with one of these disorders in the US, and if we could make a difference in a few million people's lives in our lifetimes, we felt we would leave the world a better place.

In the early summer months of 2012, Casey and Shari Childers had planned a trip to south Florida to visit family, and they decided to hit both coasts during their jaunt, just so they could stop in Jacksonville for a visit to catch up. Casey had a bit of an ulterior motive. He had mentioned that he'd met a doctor while he was at a conference. Well, not actually *met* but *stalked* a doctor after one of his presentations that week. Dr. Barry Byrne, MD, PhD, a research scientist at the University of Florida School of Medicine and the director of UF Powell Gene Therapy Center, gave a speech at the 2011 AGSCT conference held in Seattle about the process of using gene transfer therapy as a way to treat Pompe disease. The part of his speech that struck Casey like a bolt of lightning and grabbed his undivided attention was that Barry had experienced success while injecting the gene replacement vector into the diaphragm of a canine model. Knowing that the strength or lack of strength in the diaphragm of our MTM children was a huge component to the demise of our kids, Casey followed him around for a day and a half. He waited for an opportune moment to present itself to share our story of MTM.

The last thing Barry Byrne needed was another project to tend to, especially one unrelated to the disease he'd been working to cure. But, as fate would have it, Barry had that same altruistic attitude that our entire research team carried with them as their core belief. They all valued life and were focused on getting treatment to the patients to make life better for our kids. A great attitude, combined with a touch of ADD that constantly told him that he could handle one more project, ended up landing Barry in Winston Salem at WFIRM to assist Casey in injecting the MTM vector into the diaphragm of one of our canines. He'd become an integral part of the team, and Casey wanted us to meet him. At Casey's request, Barry and his wife Laura joined us for dinner in Ponte Vedra Beach.

Alison, as is typical, was intent on giving our friends a night to remember and a beautiful setting to sit and enjoy the evening. Living in Ponte Vedra Beach, Florida, it was not hard to find such a setting. A friend of Alison's owned a beautiful home on Ponte Vedra Blvd., the coveted drive along the most southern beach of Jacksonville. Alison's friend was out of town, and being generous by nature, immediately offered the use of her home for this dinner meeting. Alison planned an exquisite menu, and just a few days before Memorial Day of 2012, we all gathered at the beautiful home situated thirty yards away from the waters of the Atlantic Ocean. The night, as quiet, pleasant, and unassuming as it was, was the catalyst for the next phase of the science.

This being the first time we'd met Barry and his wife, we asked Casey to share how he'd met Barry. Casey described his excitement after hearing Barry present just six months before. Alison and I hung on every word. It was also fascinating to see Shari and Laura tune in intently; they seemed to get as much enjoyment from their husband's stories as we did. Casey and Barry didn't just swap work stories, they also shared their adventurous exploits around the globe. Exploits like Barry Byrne climbing K2 for CureDuchennes MD and Casey ascending to the summit of Mt. Rainier. These adrenaline junkies planned exciting ventures like this to counter the controlled environment of the laboratory. In the lab, they were in control, but out there on the side of these mountains, they were at the mercy of the mountain, the weather, and the integrity of the surface they planted their feet on, step after step.

The evening's discussion weaved in and out of each other's lives, from Shari sharing how Casey had convinced her to house a chocolate brown lab named Nibs for his ongoing research, to Laura's affinity for horticulture and growing exotic plants, to bits and pieces of our story about Joshua, and our journey to find a cure. As Barry learned more about our experience and realized how far our science had advanced over the last few years, he made the casual comment that we should get in touch with a guy from a life science venture capital (VC) group. Barry had been discussing the possibilities regarding his research on Pompe disease and felt he would be a good connection for us to explore as well. Barry promised to make the connection.

Barry and Laura had a ninety-minute drive back to Gainesville, and Casey and Shari were facing another five hours south to the Fort Myers/Naples area in the morning. The night ended with hugs between new friends and well wishes for the future of MTM research. Research in the last few years had advanced exponentially compared to the first ten years, and this evening's events would prove crucial to expediting our last phase of research. We left that dinner feeling encouraged about the future for our MTM kiddos.

Alison and I sat on the results of preclinical trials for nearly three years, waiting for the research, and then the writing and peer review of the paper to be completed and published. It was one of the hardest things that we've ever had to do. We couldn't tell a soul about how incredibly well the canine trials had gone and where our dogs were housed, so as not to endanger the colonies, researchers, or the advancement of the science itself. After an introduction to VC, orchestrated by Barry Byrne, Casey gave me the green light to discuss the first results of the preclinical trials which he had presented live just a month or so before in Europe.

Capitalizing on what was essentially nothing more than a warm lead from our new scientist friend Barry, I got the VC representative on the phone, and I gave a little history about Joshua and the Foundation. I told him that JFF had been involved with this research since the beginning, and we intended to see it through, hopefully alongside our chosen VC. I started touching on the actual science, and the results we were having. He calmly explained that gene transfer therapy had not been fully embraced by the venture capital community because of the history of clinical trials, one in particular, had not turned out as planned. I was very familiar with the case that he was alluding to, as I'd studied a bit of history on gene transfer therapy as our science became successful and had shown proof of concept in our mouse and dog model preclinical trials.

Prior to this success, we still had not determined our direction when it came to developing a therapeutic. We were struggling (more like agonizing) about whether to choose regenerative medicine, gene transfer therapy, or another therapy that had been thrown into the mix, protein-fusion therapy, which had proven successful in other indications. We felt it was paramount to choose the right therapy to proceed with first, because we were fighting against Father Time, and we were torn apart every time we lost another MTM warrior. One afternoon, as Alison dozed for a moment on the couch, she had a dream the answer was in the production of the protein and that it was due to a systemic administration of the gene transfer vector. Trembling, she awoke with such assurance of what needed to be done that she called Casey immediately and shared her dream. It was so real to her that she was quite shaken up, another one of those orchestrated moments. "It will be like a light switch when the protein enters the cell. It will be just a few weeks before we see the results," Alison shared.

What she didn't know is that Casey and Alan were making the decision based on research, and they were leaning heavily toward the proof of concept in Anna Buj Bello's mouse model and our dog model.

I knew and fully understood VC's hesitation, but as Alison and I believed and have said many times, this was no coincidence, and it was being orchestrated by something much bigger than we could ever imagine. We also firmly believed that eighteen months earlier, when our Joshua passed, another spirit joined that orchestration. I continued to express to the VC representative our dream of being able to find a cure for MTM, and to perpetuate funding to our scientists to go on to the next, and the next, and the next indication.

He ended the conversation warmly by commending us on all we had done and encouraging us to continue. He said he was very interested in the science and looked forward to having a discussion with Casey Childers, which was tentatively scheduled for the tenth of July, but that it was not realistic at this time to expect strong involvement from VC. "The world is not ready for Gene Therapy, keep up the good work," he said. I was encouraged that I'd been able to share our story with a representative of a major VC group over a ninety-minute conversation, but at least a little disappointed that I did not have a commitment for the hundreds of millions of dollars we knew it would take to commercialize a therapy for our children.

On July 10, Casey, the VC, and I had another long conversation. This was their first opportunity to dig deep into the science. Casey and I had forwarded some information to the VC, and he had a list of questions to delve into. The conversation, which went well beyond the one hour we intended, ended much the same way that my first call with VC had. He asked Casey to send him some respiratory information and the results Casey had experienced with the dogs, and said that he was going to get with his colleague and go over the information in great detail, but again, not to expect any immediate involvement from VC.

One of the reasons I remained hopeful through these discussions was because Casey had given me a book just a couple of months before that I read in about a day and a half. It was titled *The Forever Fix*, and it was about a boy who'd suffered from a macular degenerative genetic disorder which caused blindness by adversely affecting the rods and the cones in the eye. If I remember correctly, the boy was about four years old when he went from having perfect vision to being legally blind in just a few months. But then, the boy received a shot of gene transfer therapy in his eye, and within days, his sight returned. Interestingly, his sight returned in about the same time it took for the muscles in our dogs to double in strength. And the most important factor: there had been no immunological response to the vector. But eyes and muscles are very different when it comes to immune surveillance, so our optimism was tempered by knowing additional studies would need to be conducted. Even though VC was not ready to pump millions into gene replacement therapy, the FDA felt that science had revealed a safer vector, and I was even more hopeful for our children.

CHAPTER 31

THE WAY IS MADE

Paul

On July 23, via email, the VC representative asked Casey and I if we'd seen the news regarding gene therapy. I had not seen the news on Friday, nor had Casey or Alan Beggs or any of our scientific team stateside. Within minutes we were reading an article titled, "European Medicines Agency Recommends First Gene Therapy for Approval."

The game was about to change.

VC would begin to scramble to lock in the *low hanging fruit* of gene replacement therapy, and as fate would have it, the VC we had engaged was the only one in line for one of the first neuro-muscular diseases to be treated using a new promising vector, MTM.

The next phone conference was key in getting VC to *buy in* to the science. Alison, I, and Jon Obermeyer (a dear friend and mentor) joined the conference, from the Ponte Vedra Beach Library, where we were consulting with Jon regarding JFF. Casey joined from the University of Washington, and two of the VC team joined in from New York City. Introductions were made and for the next hour or so, the VC representatives barraged Casey with questions regarding the science. The call ended with most of their questions answered and a discussion of when they could fly out to Washington to visit Casey and more importantly, when they could see the results of the canine trials with their own eyes.

During VC's visit to Washington, Casey introduced them to Pavlov and Turing, two of Rocky's offspring who were running around like normal puppies after just one shot of gene transfer therapy using the Hind Limb Profusion. They are our rock stars and tend to make instant believers of all who meet them.

A perfect storm was brewing, and the order of events could not have been orchestrated any better. Alison and I would constantly remind each other that one higher than us was in control. These things all happened in the perfect sequence and timing, God's perfect timing.

There's a scripture that says, God's higher ways are not like our ways.

Alison and I struggled with the fact that our Josh was not here to experience this last push toward a treatment. All we could remind each other of was that His ways are not like ours, and this journey had been orchestrated since the beginning of time. Alison and I would trust God's higher ways. But the perfect storm always has some clouds. We held tight and took the time to breathe deeply and update our board members of the advancements.

There were all sorts of new components to consider as we entered this uncharted territory, as well as a million details to sift through. Alison and I were intent on protecting the institutions that had conducted the research with intellectual property (IP), and we hoped it would lead to a path of future funding for other disease states after we'd solved the MTM mysteries.

Simultaneously, Alison continued to pursue setting up calls with individuals she'd met at scientific conferences in search of the IP and connected all of us, the researchers and myself, on a call with one individual who worked on the regulatory side. At the end of one of these calls, this individual said something that stuck with Alison. "You need to be creative when thinking about the delivery process when thinking of IP."

It was weeks later, Alison sat up in the middle of the night during one of her download moments. It was either a dream or a vision, she had these throughout the years, on things in the future. She said, "The IP is in the delivery process, it's systemic application."

I looked at her and said, "What?"

She repeated, "The IP is in the delivery process." Four law firms and sixteen hours of conversations later, we found a brilliant woman attorney,

Brenda Jarrell, who also had a PhD in Biology, and in three minutes on the call, she confirmed Alison's intuitiveness.

VC did reach out to us to get the history of MTM research, and we were able to fill them in on all the details, from the institutions we had funded, to the sequence of the science. We shared that the gene had been discovered in France, and we reviewed the previous seventeen years with as much detail as we could. We needed the VC group to have a crystal-clear picture of the path to a therapy.

Months after we'd read that the first gene therapy drug had been approved in Europe, we received news we'd been waiting for since I first spoke with VC five months earlier. In months, not years, the VC representative was closing in on being ready to present to the partners and he was only going to get one shot at this presentation. Forty-five minutes after the VC rep finished his presentation, his phone rang. He noticed from the caller ID it was one of the partners of the firm. It was common for them to start having questions immediately following a presentation, so he answered the call to field a few questions. None of us were prepared for what happened next. The partners were impressed enough with the science, they proposed to give 50 percent of the Series A money needed, and it was the VC's job to find the rest. Well, after asking Alison to close the deal with another VC firm for 7.5 million, the firm found the rest of the money, and the future had never looked brighter for our MTM kiddos.

Seven months later, on a hot, sticky July afternoon when temperatures in Florida reached into the low 100s, Alison and I received an email that revolutionized our journey with MTM. In the email, the VC rep told us that he was going to finalize funding the next day and issue a press release announcing their involvement in gene therapy for MTM.

Alison and I couldn't even begin to explain the emotions we felt when we received this email. Our journey had begun on February 2, 1995, and now, nearly nineteen years later, the funding needed to take us into clinical trials was in the new company's bank account. Complete and utter jubilation came over us. I fist pumped the sky and gave a yell. We laughed, we high fived, and we began calling our scientists and congratulating them, one by one. After the last call was made, we collapsed onto our couch in the living room, and we gave each other a hug. I congratulated Alison on a job well done. The dream she'd had eighteen years before of handing a check to Tony Atala for research had culminated in an amazing feat, only accomplished by true determination and unwavering faith that God would provide an answer. Slowly, the initial excitement of the accomplishment died down a bit, and in unison, we began to honor Joshua with our thoughts. We again mourned the loss of our son. This was a special moment for us and for every MTM family across the globe. We were crying tears of joy and tears of pain simultaneously, for those gone before, and for those yet to come.

EPILOGUE

ALISON

The leaves were just beginning to turn when I found myself in Chicago in the early fall of 2017. I was there at the request of his mother. We'd gone out the night before to celebrate. If ever there was a reason to celebrate, this was it. After dinner, I returned to my hotel room to prepare for the next day, but sleep evaded me. I woke several times, worried that I'd overslept, and upon waking, thoughts of Joshua and the last twenty-two years raced through my brain. I missed Joshua fiercely that night.

***

The next morning, I woke early and arrived at the hospital a full hour early. I was prepared to be emotional, but what I felt instead was a steady calm. We were told to wait in a waiting room on the eleventh floor, while up above us, on the nineteenth floor at precisely 9:32 a.m., Noah became the first child to receive gene therapy for Myotubular Myopathy.

It took twenty-two years to get to that waiting room. Twenty-two years of vision and tenacity. Twenty-two years of heartbreak and sorrow living alongside unspeakable joy. Sixteen of those years were with my son, and six were without him beside me. I can't prove it, but I'm certain that he's been orchestrating events from heaven ever since he arrived there that Christmas Eve.

I met Noah for the first time after the injection was complete. He was calm, as if nothing had happened. By that point, I was having a hard time believing what I was watching unfold in front of me. It was surreal in the best possible way.

We named Joshua before we knew the road that awaited us. We named him after a courageous leader in the Bible, and that's what he became for the MTM community. In the weeks leading up to the injection, I began to think about Noah, and I wondered if his name was significant to this journey. As I studied, I found his name represents the symbol of an *anchor.*

An anchor of hope.

Joshua was our strong, courageous leader who brought us to this point; and Noah will be our anchor of hope. Clinical trials can be a series of stop and go points. They are, after all, a trial for safety and efficacy of the drug before it is commercialized, before it receives its Biologics License Application. Through it all, I know that there is hope. There has always been hope.

It is my hope, that by the time this book finds its way to your hands, that clinical trials are over and this drug is mainstream. Our ultimate goal is that gene therapy will change the face of MTM and will offer children the promise of life. But, if that does not happen…if for some reason clinical trials are halted and we find ourselves back at square one, I want you to know that there's hope. I want you to know that every single evening, Noah and I have a FaceTime date. I want you to know that Paul and I have seen him grow strong and happy. His muscles are developing more and more each day. We've watched him sit unassisted, we've watched him walk, and eat orally, and we're pretty sure that one of these days, he will meet the milestones of his peers. I want you to know that he's doing more with his little, tiny body than Joshua was capable of doing in sixteen years.

I want you to know that every single second of the last twenty-two years was worth it for the look on Michelle's face, Noah's mother, the day that her son received his injection. I never pictured myself walking down this road, but I would do it again in a heartbeat. I have often said, that throughout this journey, the joy outweighed the pain, that sorrow and joy are the dance of life, and if you look for the beauty, you will find it in the ashes. My life has been enriched by my journey with Joshua. I am the woman I am because my son lived.

"The foundation and Joshua's life paved the way for treatment for this fatal disorder. The science continues to be perfected...; we wait with great anticipation to see these children healed and whole. Here's to the Joshua's of the world."

Alison Rockett

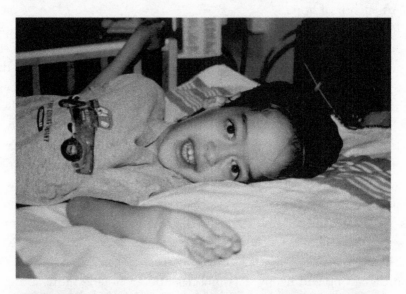

Acknowledgements

Nowhere in society does the saying, "It Takes A Village," ring truer than in the Orphan disease community. There are so many people to acknowledge who made significant impacts on our family. It would be impossible to build a comprehensive list of these people. Other than a few individuals, this acknowledgement will focus on groups of people, all important and vital to us as caregivers and dear friends.

Thank you:

Elsie Rockett (grandma): selfless and caring, helping her daughter traverse life and numerous near-death experiences early on, remaining steadfast and a pillar of strength and wisdom until her passing.

Gaspar Anastasi: our spiritual mentor and prayer warrior, petitioning for life and leading many prayer vigils in peace, hope, and love for our Joshua.

Rebecca Harvin: You are a word smith and a true friend to our family. Thank you for your help in telling Joshua's story and your loyalty through the years to our son's foundation.

The nurses and caregivers. There were many, led by "Nurse Linny" (Linda Pajank) who was with us for nearly 16 years (and part of the family). Thank you all for your love and support.

Doctors and hospital caregivers: thank you for "listening" to parents who knew the care guidelines for a disease that most of you had never heard of. Thank you for caring for our son and aiding us in navigating unknown territory.

Researchers: Thank you Doctor Anthony Atala for putting a team of world class, altruistic leaders together to push science past perceived boundaries. So much has been accomplished. We still have work to do, and we will not stop short of changing the lives of our MTM heroes.

Financial Donors: Jeff and Terry Dixon (dear friends) who wrote the first check to seed the dream of change, to my best man Pat Kelly and Syracuse University friends; Alex and Laura Zecca (Chairpersons for our fundraising events), and each and every person who wrote a check from the smallest to the largest amount. Research ushers in change, and the catalyst to our research has been your love and financial support through the years. Thank you for your continued support.

Family and Friends: The tribe begins with family and friends. Thank you for your love, acceptance, and support throughout this journey. You've made the mountain-tops attainable and the valleys liveable.

Our Myotubular Myopathy (MTM) family: We've always said this journey brings with it unbearable pain at times, but our kids bring unfathomable joy. Thank you for the joy your children have brought. Each is like one of our own children, and we love you all.

Isabella: Thank you for being the best sister. Joshua adored you. I'm glad we didn't listen to Joshua and send you back two weeks after you were born.

Blessings,
Paul, Alison, and Bella

About the Authors

Paul Frase and Alison Rockett had everything—Paul was an NFL defensive lineman; Alison was an assistant manager for Guns N' Roses and a personal assistant to fashion design mogul Max Azria, founder of BCBG.

Their first child, Joshua, was born with a muscular disorder called myotubular myopathy (MTM). The doctors would not give him more than 24 hours to live.

Alison became Joshua's advocate, and eventually the patient advocate for a whole community.

Alison taught herself how to keep her son alive and had to resuscitate him numerous times. Before Joshua had his first birthday, Alison and her husband, Paul, started a foundation that would one day find the cure for their son's disease. Knowing nothing about scientific research for a rare orphan disease, Alison educated herself and trusted her instincts. When she received a vision of handing a large check to a renowned researcher, she chased that vision with relentless passion until its fruition.

Alison has since been published in Human Gene Therapy and was featured in the MIT Technology Review. Alison has forged relationships with MDA,

NIH, NORD and Global Genes during the Joshua Frase Foundation's quest for a cure for MTM. Paul and the family were featured in USA Today during the week of Super Bowl 32, when he was a member of the Green Bay Packers squad.

Paul and Alison have been interviewed by Jerry Lee Lewis of the MDA Telethon, Jeremy Schaap on The Sporting Life, and countless other television and radio personalities and broadcasts. Paul also has been on Fox and Friends to promote the foundation.

Paul played for eleven seasons as a defensive lineman (from 1988 to 1998) with the New York Jets, Jacksonville Jaguars, Green Bay Packers, and Baltimore Ravens. He is the unprecedented two-time recipient of the Ed Block Courage award, a peer selected honor that identifies a team player who exemplifies commitment to the principles of sportsmanship and courage.

Paul's job as an NFL defensive lineman was more than just a dream job; it was the vehicle the Frases used to start their foundation, give it its much-needed publicity, and provide its initial financial backing.

One of Paul's greatest joys, however, happened off the football field. Instead of carrying a pigskin ball, he carried his precious son, Joshua, through the playground of life, one activity at a time.

The Joshua Frase Foundation website remains the largest and most comprehensive compilation of information for MTM. Please visit us at www.joshuafrase.org or Pleasedonate.org.

CPSIA information can be obtained
at www.ICGtesting.com
Printed in the USA
LVHW040205170323
741836LV00006B/279